4 129 2

UE

Changing Utilization of Fixed Capital

An Element in Long-Term Growth

Murray F. Foss

American Enterprise Institute for Public Policy Research
Washington and London

Murray F. Foss, a visiting scholar at the American Enterprise Institute, has served as a senior research associate at the National Bureau of Economic Research, as a senior staff economist with the Council of Economic Advisers, and as editor of the *Survey of Current Business*. He is the author of *Changes in the Workweek of Fixed Capital: U.S. Manufacturing, 1929 to 1976* (AEI, 1981).

Library of Congress Cataloging in Publication Data

Foss, Murray F.
 Changing utilization of fixed capital.

 1. Industrial equipment—United States—Utilization. 2. Capital—United States. 3. Hours of Labor—United States. I. Title.
HD39.3.F68   1984   332'.0414   84-9206
ISBN 0-8447-3559-0

1 3 5 7 9 10 8 6 4 2

AEI Studies 407

Printed in the United States of America

Contents

LIST OF FIGURES

Foreword

To an increasing extent long-range problems have been in the forefront of public policy debates over economic issues. Concern over government deficits in the latter part of the 1980s, the long-run financing needs of the social security system, the similar concern over Medicare, the debate over the desirability of what has come to be known as "industrial policy"—all these are problems that require us to look beyond this year or next. Taking the long view is no less important for a better understanding of how our economy works.

Although we look to the long-run growth of productivity to provide us with rising living standards, we still have much to learn about what has caused productivity to increase. Investigators of past productivity growth have invariably come up with a large undigested chunk that has been labeled "technological change" or "increase in knowledge"—or "unexplained residual."

In the past, investigators of our nation's economic growth have made no allowance for the fact that our nation's plant and equipment are being utilized more intensively than in the past because of the spread of late shifts. In 1981 the American Enterprise Institute published a study by Murray F. Foss that showed that manufacturing plants worked 25 percent more hours in a normal week in 1976 than they did in 1929—despite the fact that an average employee worked a much shorter week. The present study demonstrates that this is a continuing development rather than a one-shot occurrence and it is a development that may be found not only in manufacturing but in the nonfarm business economy as a whole. This demonstration means that the effect of longer hours for the stock of fixed capital makes up an identifiable part of the growth in productivity as now measured. The study also demonstrates that in examining key ratios like the ratio of capital to production or that of capital to labor, more meaningful ratios are obtained when taking account of changes in the workweek of capital.

The findings of the present study impinge on such questions as, Do we save and invest enough as a nation? Basic research of this kind also contributes to public policy formation by adding to our understanding of how the economy operates.

WILLIAM J. BAROODY, JR.
President
American Enterprise Institute

Preface

The number of hours per week worked by the average person in the labor force has declined over the long run and has continued to decline even though the forty-hour week became the standard in this country after the end of World War II. Observing this behavior of the labor workweek, students of U.S. economic growth have raised questions about the behavior of average weekly hours worked by fixed capital. In 1981 the American Enterprise Institute published a study of mine that showed that the number of hours per week worked by manufacturing plants, rather than falling, increased by some 25 percent from 1929 to 1976, as a result of an increase in late-shift work. The first study presented figures for only two years for manufacturing. This study fills in the statistical void between 1929 and 1976 and extends the investigation to sectors outside manufacturing. Although the data for some industries leave much to be desired, the overall results have a large solid core. In any case, the study should be viewed as a beginning in areas either unexplored or little explored in the United States.

These statistics have significance for the way capital is used in this country, for productivity and its growth, and for the growth of output. The utilization of capital has been a topic of interest to economists for some time; indeed, the present study can be viewed as an outgrowth of a study of utilization I did more than twenty years ago.[1] Coming at a time that saw the appearance of major works on the nation's long-term economic growth by Kendrick, Denison, and others, my early investigation gave rise to what I have called the "capital utilization controversy" from the mid-1960s to the early 1970s.[2] Major new books on shift work have appeared in recent years.[3] At the meetings of the American Economic Association in September 1980, a session was devoted to the economics of slack capacity,[4] the subject of a recent book by Gordon Winston.[5]

Although interest in capital utilization has led to active discussion among economists, research on the subject of changing capital utilization in this country at least has been relatively meager. The earlier capital utilization controversy was tabled in effect for lack of data. The main contribution of this book is the information it provides. This study finds that the rise in the workweek of fixed capital in manufacturing documented in my first AEI study has not been a one-time phenomenon but has been part of a continuing trend, which has manifested varying rates of change over the past half-century or so. The workweek of capital of other industries taken as a group has also increased since the end of World War II, although much less than in manufacturing. These findings are a confirmation of a rather common development in this country—the spread of shift work—but a development that economists have largely ignored until recently. These results mean that some of the long-term rise in "total factor productivity" stems from a longer workweek of the capital stock. They are one manifestation of how business has economized in its use of capital in the past, and they shed at least a little new light on productivity growth. where much light remains to be shed.

Whether this kind of economizing on capital will continue in the future will depend on several factors, such as the trend of technology and the added variable costs of operating capital facilities on late shifts. For example, technological developments like the spread of the small, low-cost computer as a substitute for large, costly computers in private business reduces the economic incentive for shift work.

The findings of the study have implications for public policy. For example, a basic tenet of economic policy of the present administration has been the notion that saving in this country has been too low because of excessive taxation and as a consequence fixed investment has been discouraged. A nation that uses its fixed capital efficiently through late-shift work, like the United States, may to that extent be able to tolerate a lower saving rate. This is not the only aspect of economizing on capital. It has been said in the many comparisons between Japan and this country that the Japanese utilize their factory machinery much more effectively than we do.[6] They are said to take more care than U.S. businessmen in training their workers to become familiar with new equipment. Knowing more about such topics would provide a stronger basis for public policy regarding capital formation.

The main findings and their significance appear in chapter 1. Chapters 2 and 3 are devoted to manufacturing; the former chapter discusses the estimating procedure, and the latter examines the reasonableness of the manufacturing results and the major economic influences on the development of shift work, especially in the period from 1929 to the early post–World War II period. The rest of the study deals with estimation, but the reader may find some of the statistics of interest. Chapter 4 is devoted to those nonmanufacturing industries where the data are most reliable: continuous industries, mining, and retail trade. The fifth and last chapter is devoted to computers and the ways they have affected hours worked by office equipment. Specific appendixes deal with the derivation of overall totals, various nonmanufacturing industries, alternative weighting in the derivation of the overall results, and capital-labor ratios in manufacturing.

Notes

1. Murray F. Foss, "The Utilization of Capital Equipment," *Survey of Current Business*, vol. 43 (June 1963), pp. 8–16.

2. See *Survey of Current Business: The Measurement of Productivity*, vol. 52, no. 5, part 2 (May 1972).

3. Roger R. Betancourt and Christopher K. Clague, *Capital Utilization: A Theoretical and Empirical Analysis* (New York: Cambridge University Press, 1981).

4. The session "Economics of Slack Capacity" included the following papers: Ernst R. Berndt and Catherine J. Morrison, "Capacity Utilization Measures: Underlying Economic Theory and an Alternative Approach"; Arthur De Vany and N. G. Frey, "Stochastic Equilibrium and Capacity Utilization"; Murray F. Foss, "Long-Run Changes in the Workweek of Fixed Capital"; and Walter Y. Oi, "Slack Capacity: Productive or Wasteful?" *American Economic Review, Papers and Proceedings*, vol. 71, no. 2 (May 1981), pp. 48–69.

5. Gordon C. Winston, *The Timing of Economic Activities: Firms, Households and Markets, and Time-Specific Analysis* (New York: Cambridge University Press, 1982).

6. Robert H. Hayes, "Why Japanese Factories Work," *Harvard Business Review* (July–August 1981), pp. 57–66.

Acknowledgments

This study was supported by a grant from the National Science Foundation as well as by the American Enterprise Institute. I am indebted to Marvin Kosters and Martin Marimont for having read the manuscript. I also owe a debt to a number of individuals in private business for information and advice about their industries. I alone am responsible for errors and shortcomings.

I owe thanks to several people for research assistance: Nancy Bordeaux, Robert Dubman, Laurel Gillis, Scott Innis, Denise Ruggeri, and especially Beatrice Goley. I also wish to thank Lucille Jones for having typed most of the manuscript.

1
Introduction and Main Findings

This investigation of changes in weekly hours worked by manufacturing plants, mines, retail stores, and other kinds of privately owned fixed capital for the years between 1929 and 1976 is a sequel to my study *Changes in the Workweek of Fixed Capital: U.S. Manufacturing, 1929 to 1976*, which the American Enterprise Institute published in early 1981. Using data from the Bureau of the Census, that study presented estimates of average weekly hours of operation of manufacturing plants, by industry, for two years: 1929 and 1976. It found that operating hours of plants had increased by some 25 percent over this span of almost half a century even though the workweek of labor was shorter; that most industries, whether defined broadly or in detail, had experienced increases, some of which were quite large; and that few industries had experienced decreases. No estimates were provided for interim years, however, nor were any findings presented for industries other than manufacturing. These are the two main gaps the present investigation seeks to fill.

The comparison of 1976 with 1929 in the first study proved to be informative but left unresolved whether changes in average weekly plant hours are still going on or whether the changes occurred several decades ago and are now largely over. Similarly, can the findings for the manufacturing sector be generalized to the rest of the business economy? The private sector outside manufacturing embraces important industries, like electric and gas utilities and the telephone system, that operate continuously. These industries, which are highly capital intensive, have experienced no change in their hours of operation for the period covered. We know, however, that retail stores keep longer hours than they used to and that some kinds of office work, like that performed by large computers, are carried out on a schedule of twenty-four hours per day. In contrast, some industries, like contract construction and a broad array of service industries, now operate fewer hours per week than formerly. The problem is to bring information pertaining to various parts of the economy together into an overall figure.

1

Answers to these questions are of interest for several reasons. They can finally shed some light on a question posed by earlier investigators, namely, whether the decline of weekly hours worked by labor in the past half-century or so has been accompanied by a decline in hours worked by capital. More generally, these questions have a bearing on the growth of the nation's output and productivity. Here I am referring not to the widely publicized discussion of the slowdown in productivity growth since the mid-1960s or early 1970s but to some of the broader facts about growth that have come to light in the past twenty-five or thirty years.

The numerous investigations of output growth in the United States have come to the same principal conclusions. First, output has grown more rapidly than the weighted input of labor and capital (and land) combined. The difference is a reflection of the growth in productivity.[1]

In a recent publication the Bureau of Labor Statistics (BLS) presented figures showing that the ratio of productivity growth to output growth from 1948 to 1973 was large in spite of differences among investigators: 32 percent on the basis of Dale Jorgenson's estimates; 54 percent for the BLS; 56 percent for Edward Denison; and 62 percent for John Kendrick.[2] Productivity growth has been found important not only for the private economy as a whole but also for major industry divisions like manufacturing, for major manufacturing industries,[3] and for earlier time periods.[4]

A second finding is that the role of fixed capital (construction and equipment) in output growth, though significant, has not been of overriding importance.[5] In studies of output growth the importance of factors of production is measured by the income or output they produce. Not only is the nonlabor share much smaller than the labor share, but it has not increased over the long run. Furthermore, the nonlabor share of income or output must be divided among several kinds of capital—inventories and land, as well as plant and equipment. This is not to suggest that there are few differences among investigators about how to measure the importance of capital. For example, for the postwar period Dale Jorgenson assigns a weight to capital that is about double the weight assigned by Edward Denison. Investigators also differ in how they measure changes in capital input, a topic of particular importance for purposes of the present study.[6] Typically capital input has been measured by the stock of capital in place or available—or by the flow of services from that stock; changes in capital input over time have been measured by changes in such a stock or its services from one period to another. Conventional measures of capital have not reflected changes in fixed capital's workweek

2

in measured capital input. With conventional measures the effect on output of any changes in the workweek of capital would be reflected in the change in total factor productivity.

The third broad finding is that economists disagree about what lies behind the long-term growth in productivity. The difference between the growth of output and the growth of input has been given many designations, among others, technical progress, total factor productivity, or the residual. But whatever it has been called, economists have been disturbed by their lack of understanding of so large a component of output growth. As Moses Abramovitz observed more than twenty-five years ago: "In a sense it is sobering if not discouraging . . . that we know so little of the causes of technical progress or the residual. . . . The indicated importance of this element may be taken as a measure of our ignorance about the causes of economic growth."[7] In September 1983, the BLS, in presenting its new estimates of multifactor productivity, could not avoid making the same point.[8]

Between the time Abramovitz published his study and the present there has been an outpouring of investigations of productivity growth. Since the earliest studies many investigators have whittled down the size of the residual by taking account of factors not captured by crude input measures, such as man-hours. Thus labor has become better educated; and, since there is considerable evidence that returns to education are reflected in higher levels of hourly wages and salaries, an adjustment is often made for the increased educational attainment of the labor force in the measure of labor input. Although these and other adjustments have increased the relative importance of measured kinds of input—both labor and capital—in accounting for output growth, sizable residuals remain.

Denison has pioneered in making quantitative estimates of the various influences underlying the growth of productivity, after making numerous adjustments to input. He has attributed private productivity growth in the United States from 1948 to 1973 to three main influences: the shift of resources off farms into more productive nonfarm uses; economies of scale attributable to the increase in the size of markets; and the "increase in knowledge."[9] The last item, an approach to what many economists and other investigators have called "technical progress," embraces in the Denison scheme not only technical change but also management's increase in knowledge and skill. Some of these influences can be measured more successfully than others. The increase in knowledge, for example, is inherently not measurable and in Denison's system, as in most others, is a residual.

Nestor Terleckyj and John Kendrick attempted to explain productivity growth in individual manufacturing industries by a number of factors but did not have striking success.[10] Their factors included such things as the rate of output growth, the cyclical variability of output, and research and development (R & D) outlays. The trouble with output growth is that one does not know how the causation runs— from output growth to productivity growth or the other way around. The cyclical variability explanation lacks a strong theory. In this type of industry analysis the R & D variable yielded mixed results. Richard Nelson and Sidney Winter, however, found R & D to be an important variable in explaining productivity growth across industries.[11]

The R & D variable, which in some respects might be described as everyone's favorite, is a good example of an influence thought to be important for productivity growth but hard to measure; indeed, according to some investigators, it has only a tenuous connection to productivity growth. Denison, for example, remains a skeptic—not about research but about R & D expenditures as they relate to productivity growth. Nor have detailed R & D studies at the micro level, like those by Edwin Mansfield and by Zvi Griliches, escaped criticism.[12] A 1979 report on productivity by the National Academy of Sciences, for example, states that "industrial R & D has probably been an important source of productivity advance for the economy as a whole. However, the data underlying these studies are imprecise."[13] Education is now given considerable importance in accounting for growth, and most investigators now adjust crude labor input like man-hours to reflect changes in educational attainment. Yet at a 1982 AEI conference Theodore Schultz, who was among the first to emphasize the role of education in economic growth, acknowledged that the relation is subtle and not well understood.[14] Richard Nelson summed up this state of affairs as follows: "If this measure of our ignorance is not completely mysterious, it certainly is not well understood."[15]

Clearly establishing close connections between productivity growth and the factors responsible for it is important. When we discuss a longer workweek of capital, we are talking about a measurable influence whose effect on productivity is direct. To the extent that we can pinpoint specific influences of this sort, our understanding of productivity growth is enhanced.

The pages that follow will show that mainly as a result of shift work, the workweek of capital expanded during the 1930s in manufacturing and has continued to increase in the post–World War II period. Indeed, from 1952 to 1979 employment of production workers on *late* shifts in noncontinuous industries, where some shift work is usually found, accounted for seven-eighths of the *total* rise in production worker employment in manufacturing over this period. The growth of late-shift employment in such industries was even relatively more

4

important in the 1970s. The use of multiple shifts has been the dominant mode of factory production in the postwar period.

The workweek of capital in the nonfarm business sector has risen from 1929 as well as from the early post–World War II period to the mid–1970s. Although the rise in the workweek of the total nonfarm capital stock is much smaller than that observed in manufacturing alone, it is significant that these long-run changes are positive and not, as has often been thought, negative like the workweek of labor. The significance of this finding is that a small but measurable part of the increase in total factor productivity can be accounted for by the lengthening of capital's workweek. In a growth-accounting framework the contribution of plant and equipment can be thought of as somewhat greater than is otherwise apparent.

Some Basic Concepts

The number of hours per week a business establishment is ordinarily open and operating is an aspect of a firm's investment decision. For example, when deciding to build a new plant or expand an existing one, the firm can choose a larger plant operating fewer hours per week or a smaller plant operating more hours to achieve a given output. Since the legislation of the 1930s requiring premium pay for labor overtime, changes in weekly plant hours in the United States have come about mainly because of an increase in shift work.

These two considerations—the amount of capital and the number of hours or shifts it is scheduled to run in a week—are both relevant dimensions for the measurement of capital. Of course, as demand changes over the business cycle, a firm may also alter the number of shifts it works, although in practice alterations of this type are not frequent in most industries, motor vehicles being an important exception.[16] In any case, the focus of this study is on long-run aspects and not on short-run, cyclical fluctuations.

The decision of a firm to use shift work or otherwise to lengthen its normal operating hours is a form of economizing on capital that depends on certain microeconomic considerations as well as on certain institutional factors. For the microtheory, economists are indebted to Robin Marris, Gordon Winston, and Roger Betancourt and Christopher Clague.[17] The greater the capital intensity of production, the greater the incentive to use shift work. Running extra shifts, however, may entail increases in marginal costs, the most important of which is labor. Premiums are ordinarily paid for work on second or third shifts, but other costs, such as lighting and heating, may also be involved. Shift work is encouraged when the price of capital is high in relation

5

to the price of labor, and the use of it depends also on the ease with which capital can be substituted for labor in response to a decline in the relative price of capital. In small businesses the hours of operation are often limited by management; ultimately this may be viewed as a choice between income and leisure on the part of the small businessman.

If capital intensity encourages shift work, a change in technology in the direction of capital intensity or a change in relative prices that leads to the substitution of capital for labor—or both—will foster shift work. However desirable distinguishing between those two possibilities may be, for purposes of this particular study that distinction does not seem to be necessary. In a similar vein it would be interesting to know why, in the face of an increased demand for late-shift workers, late-shift wage differentials in manufacturing have decreased in relation to straight-time wages over the past twenty years or more. Whether the decrease reflects a changed attitude by labor toward working at night or a reduction in the real costs of night work because of improved transportation and improved amenities available in factories, it seems reasonable to suppose that the relative decline in late-shift wage differentials has fostered the growth in shift work since the late 1950s.

Consumer habits may also affect hours of operation. For a variety of reasons, such as the increased participation of women in the labor force and the increase in persons employed on late shifts, retail stores now operate longer hours than they did. By the same token, television and radio stations operate a greater part of a twenty-four-hour day than in the past. Employment regulations pertaining to women may have limited shift work formerly, but regulations of this sort seem to have little force at present as a result of the trend toward equality between the sexes. In the past, blue laws affected the number of days a store could be open or the hours when entertainment was publicly available. The decreasing force of such laws has fostered a longer week for both retail stores and spectator sports.

Two Kinds of Changes in Capital Hours. Several years ago I conducted a study that found that hours per year worked per unit of capital equipment in manufacturing (and in other sectors as well) had increased from the late 1920s to the mid-1950s.[18] I did not know why the increase had occurred but speculated that an increase in shift work was one reason for it. Although the present study is concerned primarily with shift work, analytically it is possible to distinguish another kind of change in hours per week or per year worked per unit of capital, namely, changes in hours that come about from more efficient use of capital by management *with the shift pattern held constant.*[19] Management may discover methods of operating particular machines longer hours, thereby reducing idle machine time and decreasing the need for additional investment. Greater ability to use the machines may come about in innumerable ways—for example, by rearranging plant layout, by changing the product mix or lot size, or by reducing hours for maintenance labor through the use of, say, a superior lubricant. This kind of increase in capital efficiency may come about also as labor becomes more familiar with new machinery in a "learning by doing" process or by discovery of new uses for equipment, as discussed in chapter 5 in connection with computers. Or the existence of indivisibilities can give rise to an increase in capital efficiency over time. Some types of capital are needed for production regardless of the scale of production, but often the minimum size of the capital far exceeds initial needs. As output rises over time, the indivisible unit of capital may be used with increased efficiency.[20] These are just a few examples.

When capital is measured by available capital in place or by the flow of services from it, the effect on output of any change in average weekly capital hours is subsumed under the change in total factor productivity regardless of how the change in weekly capital hours comes about—whether from a change in the workweek of capital or from more efficient use of capital by management with shift work held constant. In the present study I show the importance of the rise in the workweek of capital in the growth of productivity and output. But I also present (in table 7) some estimates of the importance of this lengthening in the workweek of capital in the increase in annual hours worked per unit of equipment in manufacturing, as revealed in my earliest study.

Results

Total Nonfarm Industries. The main results of this study are presented in table 1, which gives indexes of average weekly hours worked by fixed capital, annually, from 1929 to 1976. Summary statistics based on table 1 are presented in table 2 in the form of average rates of change compounded annually.

Average weekly hours worked by fixed capital in the private nonfarm business economy (excluding nonprofit organizations) rose at a compounded annual rate of 0.18 percent from 1929 to 1976. Over this period the growth of fixed capital in this same sector was 2.24 percent per year, so that the growth in capital hours constituted 8 percent of the growth in stock (see table 2). Most of the rise in capital hours was

TABLE 1

Indexes of Average Weekly Hours of Fixed Capital, by Industry Division, 1929–1976
(1929 = 100)

	Total Nonfarm Business	Manufacturing	Mining[a]	Retail Trade	Wholesale Trade	Services	Construction	Finance and Insurance	TV and Radio	Continuous Non-manufacturing	Office Equipment
1954 weights	100.0	33.1	1.0	6.0	1.8	5.5	1.3	1.9	0.1	48.5	0.8
1929	100.0	100.0	100.0	100.0	100.0	100.0	100.0	100.0	100.0	100.0	100.0
1930	100.2	100.8	99.5	99.7	100.0	99.8	97.2	99.5	101.2	100.0	99.5
1931	100.3	101.4	98.9	99.7	100.2	99.7	96.0	98.8	102.4	100.0	98.8
1932	100.5	102.1	98.6	99.7	100.2	99.5	94.3	98.1	103.6	100.0	98.1
1933	100.8	103.2	97.5	99.5	100.4	99.3	94.0	97.6	104.7	100.0	97.6
1934	100.6	102.8	96.8	99.5	100.4	99.2	90.5	97.2	105.9	100.0	97.2
1935	101.0	104.2	96.2	99.4	100.6	99.0	89.8	96.5	107.1	100.0	96.5
1936	101.2	104.9	95.5	99.4	100.6	98.9	89.8	95.8	108.3	100.0	95.8
1937	101.4	105.6	94.9	99.4	100.8	98.6	90.2	95.3	109.4	100.0	95.3
1938	101.6	106.4	94.7	99.2	100.9	98.5	88.7	94.8	110.6	100.0	94.8
1939	101.8	107.0	94.2	99.2	100.9	98.4	88.5	94.1	111.9	100.0	94.1
1940	102.0	107.6	93.9	99.2	101.1	98.2	88.4	93.4	113.0	100.0	93.4
1941	102.3	108.5	94.6	99.2	101.1	98.4	88.8	92.9	113.5	100.0	92.9
1942	102.6	109.3	95.0	99.2	101.3	98.3	89.5	92.5	113.9	100.0	92.5
1943	102.8	110.0	95.8	99.4	101.5	98.2	89.4	91.7	114.3	100.0	91.7
1944	103.0	110.6	96.9	99.5	101.7	98.2	89.5	91.0	114.7	100.0	91.0
1945	103.2	111.4	98.2	99.5	101.7	98.2	89.5	90.6	115.2	100.0	90.6

1946	103.3	111.5	99.4	99.7	101.9	98.1	88.7	90.1	115.6	100.0	90.1
1947	103.4	111.8	100.1	99.7	102.1	98.0	88.6	89.4	116.0	100.0	89.4
1948	103.4	112.0	100.9	99.8	102.3	97.9	88.6	89.4	116.5	100.0	89.4
1949	103.5	112.2	101.6	99.8	102.3	97.8	88.7	89.2	116.9	100.0	89.2
1950	103.6	112.5	102.0	100.0	102.3	98.1	88.8	88.9	117.4	100.0	88.9
1951	103.7	112.7	101.8	100.0	102.5	98.0	88.7	88.9	117.7	100.0	88.9
1952	103.8	113.0	102.7	100.2	102.5	97.8	88.7	89.2	118.2	100.0	88.9
1953	103.9	113.3	103.1	100.2	102.5	97.6	88.7	88.9	118.6	100.0	88.9
1954	104.0	113.5	104.4	100.3	102.6	97.8	88.7	88.7	121.1	100.0	88.9
1955	104.2	113.9	104.7	100.5	102.8	97.8	88.7	88.7	123.5	100.0	87.4
1956	104.2	114.1	105.3	100.8	103.2	97.8	88.7	87.0	125.9	100.0	91.5
1957	104.4	114.4	105.7	100.9	103.4	97.6	88.7	86.6	128.4	100.0	93.5
1958	104.5	114.6	107.0	101.1	103.6	97.6	88.6	87.5	130.8	100.0	97.1
1959	104.6	114.8	107.7	101.2	103.8	97.8	88.6	88.0	133.3	100.0	99.7
1960	104.7	114.9	108.2	101.4	104.0	97.8	88.5	87.7	135.7	100.0	104.3
1961	105.0	115.7	108.7	101.5	104.3	97.6	88.4	87.0	136.5	100.0	111.5
1962	105.3	116.4	109.5	101.8	104.5	97.5	88.3	88.0	137.2	100.0	112.0
1963	105.6	117.1	110.0	102.2	104.7	97.4	88.1	88.4	138.0	100.0	119.7
1964	106.0	117.9	110.3	102.5	104.9	97.3	88.1	88.0	138.7	100.0	128.5
1965	106.4	118.6	111.0	102.8	105.3	97.1	88.0	87.7	139.5	100.0	141.3
1966	106.7	119.4	111.7	103.1	105.5	96.7	88.0	88.0	140.3	100.0	151.1
1967	107.0	120.2	112.3	103.4	105.7	96.3	87.9	87.5	141.0	100.0	162.4
1968	107.4	120.8	112.7	103.7	105.9	96.1	87.9	87.3	141.8	100.0	173.2
1969	107.7	121.6	113.4	104.1	106.2	95.9	88.0	87.5	142.5	100.0	181.9
1970	107.9	122.1	115.0	104.5	106.4	95.4	87.8	86.6	143.3	100.0	189.1
1971	108.1	122.4	116.8	104.8	107.0	95.2	87.7	86.3	144.1	100.0	194.8

(Table continues)

9

TABLE 1 (continued)

	Total Nonfarm Business	Manu- facturing	Mining[a]	Retail Trade	Whole- sale Trade	Services	Con- struction	Finance and Insurance	TV and Radio	Contin- uous Non- manufacturing	Office Equip- ment
1972	108.4	122.9	117.0	105.4	107.4	95.1	87.7	86.3	144.9	100.0	199.9
1973	108.6	123.4	117.4	105.5	107.8	94.8	87.5	86.3	145.7	100.0	210.2
1974	108.7	123.8	118.8	105.4	108.3	94.4	87.5	86.1	146.5	100.0	212.2
1975	108.8	124.2	119.2	105.8	108.7	94.1	87.7	86.1	147.3	100.0	204.0
1976	109.0	124.7	119.9	106.1	109.1	93.9	87.7	85.8	148.1	100.0	208.1

a. Excludes crude petroleum.

SOURCE: Author.

TABLE 2

GROWTH RATES IN FIXED CAPITAL AND IN AVERAGE WEEKLY CAPITAL
HOURS, NONFARM BUSINESS AND MANUFACTURING, 1929–1976
(average percent per year)

	Capital (1)	Hours (2)	Capital + Hours	Hours as Percentage of Capital[a]
	Nonfarm Business			
1929–1976	2.24	0.18	2.42	8.0
1929–1948	0.15	0.18	0.33	120.0
1948–1976	3.68	0.19	3.87	5.2
1948–1959	3.25	0.11	3.36	3.4
1959–1969	3.91	0.30	4.21	7.7
1969–1976	4.02	0.17	4.19	4.2
	Manufacturing			
1929–1976	2.30	0.47	2.77	20.4
1929–1948	1.00	0.60	1.60	60.0
1948–1976	3.19	0.38	3.57	11.9
1948–1959	3.39	0.22	3.61	6.5
1959–1969	3.11	0.58	3.69	18.6
1969–1976	2.99	0.36	3.35	12.0
1969–1979	3.44	0.36	3.80	10.5

a. Column 2 ÷ column 1 × 100.

SOURCES: Capital: Gross stocks of plant and equipment in 1972 prices from John C. Musgrave, "Fixed Capital Stocks in the United States: Revised Estimates," *Survey of Current Business*, vol. 61, no. 2 (February 1981), p. 59, table 3, and "Fixed Reproducible Tangible Wealth in the United States, 1979–82," *Survey of Current Business*, vol. 63, no. 8 (August 1983), p. 62, table 3. Totals for manufacturing and nonfarm nonmanufacturing combined were reduced by plant and equipment stocks of nonprofit organizations (unpublished BEA estimates). Data exclude residential capital. Hours: See table 1.

accounted for by manufacturing. All of these results are based on the use of constant weights for fixed capital by industry and not on changes in the mix of industries.[21]

From 1929 to 1948, the overall change in average weekly capital hours was the same as the average change from 1929 to 1976, with a rise in the manufacturing workweek of capital offsetting a decline in the workweek of other industries. The gross stock of capital grew very little over this period, however, because of the depression and then World War II. Indeed, for this earlier period the growth in average weekly capital hours was about as large as the growth of the stock.

Over the postwar period, 1948–1976, the fixed capital stock grew at an annual rate of 3.68 percent. The annual growth in weekly capital hours of 0.19 percent was about 5 percent of this growth. The average annual change in hours was slow from 1948 to 1959, but it accelerated from 1959 to 1969 and then slowed down again. During the 1960s the change in hours constituted more than 7½ percent of the stock change.

Appendix F presents some all-industry results with a different weighting system. The use of capital weights that remain fixed for a decade or so and then change would alter the results a little: the growth rate in the length of the workweek of capital for the entire period would not change much, but the average annual rate of increase for the postwar period as a whole would be somewhat higher than that for the prewar period.

Manufacturing. On the basis of fixed weights, the average annual rate of increase in the workweek of capital over the entire forty-seven-year period was much greater in manufacturing than in private nonfarm business—0.47 percent versus 0.18 percent. In contrast to the overall results, however, the average annual rate of increase in manufacturing was apparently much greater for the earlier period than for the postwar period: 0.60 percent per year versus 0.38 percent (see table 2, bottom).

During the postwar period the pattern of change in average weekly plant hours in manufacturing in a rough way paralleled the all-industry pattern. From 1948 to the end of the 1950s, weekly hours changed relatively little, but the rate of increase accelerated in the 1960s and then slowed down. The retardation seems much less, however, in manufacturing than overall.

No reliable information concerning the change in average weekly hours in manufacturing as a whole could be found for the interval from 1929 to 1948. Since I started this research with manufacturing figures for 1929 and 1976 and was able to work backward from 1976 to 1948, the estimate for the 1929–1948 period is treated as a residual.

The rise in weekly hours worked by plants has augmented a substantial increase in the stock of manufacturing capital. From 1948 to 1976 the lengthening in plant hours on an annual basis was about 12 percent of the annual increase in the stock of fixed capital. From 1929 to 1948, however, the ratio was 60 percent because the plant workweek was rising rapidly at a time when the gross stock of capital was growing very slowly. In the post–World War II period the ratio was least in the 1950s (6.5 percent) and greatest in the 1960s (18.6 percent). Indeed the slowdown in the growth of the manufacturing

FIGURE 1

Capital-Output Ratios in Manufacturing, 1948–1976

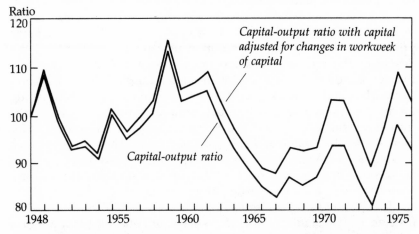

SOURCES: (1) Output indexes are based on GDP in constant dollars (1972) from BEA, *The National Income and Product Accounts of the United States, 1929–76 Statistical Tables,* table 6.2, line 9, p. 228. (2) Index of capital hours is from table 1. (3) Index of capital = gross stocks of plant and equipment in 1972 dollars from BEA. (4) Index of capital adjusted for changes in workweek of capital is (2) × (3).

Capital-output ratio = (3) ÷ (1).
Adjusted capital-output ratio = (4) ÷ (1).

capital stock from the 1950s to the 1960s—from 3.4 percent to 3.1 percent per year—would approximately disappear if an allowance were made for the rise in the plant workweek. In fact, if the data were extended to 1979, there is a suggestion of a slight acceleration in the average annual growth of the manufacturing capital stock adjusted for hours in each of the three decades from 1948 to 1979, as the second column of table 1 indicates.

The increase from 1929 to 1976 in average weekly plant hours in manufacturing as a whole would be greater if not for the fact that a large part of the capital stock in manufacturing has always operated continuously through the day and week. Omitting this portion as well as industries that have always operated a single shift yields a greater increase over the forty-seven years—32 percent rather than 25 percent—for that part of the manufacturing stock for which increased shift work has been an important option.

Measured by stocks of plant and equipment alone, capital-output ratios declined at an annual rate of 0.3 percent from 1948 to 1976 but rose a little (0.1 percent) when stocks are adjusted by the change in the average workweek of capital (see figure 1). The capital-labor ratio rose 3.3 percent before this adjustment and 3.7 percent after the adjustment. (Labor input is measured by BLS estimates of hours worked by all persons in manufacturing.)

A longer workweek of capital appears to be a response to the increased capital intensity of production in the postwar years, relative price trends favoring the substitution of capital for labor, and the desire on the part of management to use capital more efficiently through multiple-shift work. This trend to multiple shifts was accompanied by—and was itself a cause of—the trend in manufacturing production away from small firms toward large firms. At the start of the period, single-unit firms consisting of a single plant accounted for more than half of value added in manufacturing. The proportion was down to 32 percent by the mid-1950s and to 17 percent in 1977. Owners of small firms work long hours but apparently value their leisure since they tend not to use extra shifts.

The trend of wage differentials—since the late 1950s at least—has fostered longer plant hours since wage differentials for second- and third-shift work have not kept pace with wages generally. Indeed, from the end of World War II to the late 1950s a *rising* trend of wage differentials may have hampered the lengthening of weekly capital hours.

After 1960 a lengthening of plant hours occurred in all the major regions of the country except the West. It was most pronounced in the North Central states, at least until the middle 1970s. Some rise occurred in the West in the 1960s, but subsequent decreases offset these earlier rises. The national rise in average plant hours in the early period (1929–1948) seems to be associated with the movement of industry to the South.

As important as the rise in the workweek of manufacturing capital has been since 1929, other factors have also led to greater intensity of capital equipment use. From 1929 to the mid-1960s these other factors—"management improvements"—were apparently even more important than the rise in the workweek of capital.

Nonmanufacturing. Nonmanufacturing can be divided into two parts. The larger part, which includes the public utilities as well as crude petroleum and natural gas and hotels and hospitals, operates around the clock through the year. The hours for these industries by definition have not changed. In 1954—which is about midway between 1929 and 1976—fixed capital in these industries constituted 51 percent of total gross stocks of fixed nonfarm business capital and 72 percent of total nonfarm nonmanufacturing stocks.

The remainder of nonmanufacturing shows mixed trends. A rise

14

in average hours worked in coal mining reflects two main developments: (1) Strip mining has accounted for an increasing share of output, and strip mines have tended to work longer hours than underground mines. (2) The rise in capital intensity of underground coal mining has been accompanied by increasing use of multiple shifts. Important equipment, like continuous mining machines, is now operated on an around-the-clock basis.

There has been a slow but fairly steady rise in weekly hours worked by retail stores, which is partly a reflection of changed shopping habits of consumers and is associated with the increased participation of women in the labor force. Although the individual small retail business owner has always worked a long week, his numbers are steadily diminishing as chains have taken over an increasing share of the market. With a larger proportion of the labor force now employed on evening shifts, radio and television stations now broadcast longer hours than in the past, although the desire on the part of the station to reduce capital costs per unit is doubtless a factor.

There is little information for other nonmanufacturing industries. It is fairly likely that hours worked in warehouses have increased slightly, but decreases accompanying the decline in the workweek of labor are suggested in contract construction, finance, and services.

Office Equipment and Computers. The approach outlined above is an industry approach that could not capture the spread in the use of large computers over the past thirty years or so. The computers for the most part have taken the place of more conventional equipment like adding machines, typewriters, and so forth. Because of the high cost of large computers, businesses tend to operate them long weekly hours, far in excess of the forty hours that conventional equipment is available for use. This shift to large computers is responsible for a 133 percent increase in hours worked by office equipment as a whole from 1948 to 1976. The development and rapid growth of low-cost small computers, however, may well be starting to reverse the postwar trend of rising average weekly capital hours in the computer field.

Significance of Results

One way of gauging the importance of shift work is to ask how much greater the stock of capital might be if it were not for longer capital hours. At the end of 1976 the gross stock of capital in private nonfarm business (excluding housing) was $2.5 trillion in current prices. If 1976 hours worked by capital were no higher than in 1929, the stock would have to be $200 billion greater (0.08 × 2.5 trillion). This would have required a corresponding increase in gross saving since 1929.

Growth-Accounting Framework. Another way of judging the rise in capital hours is in terms of the growth-accounting framework that underlies much of the discussion about output and productivity growth over the last two decades or so.[22] In a growth-accounting framework the contribution made by a determinant of growth to the growth of output over a particular period depends on two things: its importance or weight and its rate of increase. Weights show returns to labor and capital as reflected in the income or output produced by a sector or an industry. An illustration for manufacturing is given in table 3.

TABLE 3

CONTRIBUTION TO THE GROWTH OF MANUFACTURING OUTPUT: LABOR INPUT, CAPITAL INPUT, AND TOTAL FACTOR PRODUCTIVITY, 1948–1976

	1962 Weight (%)	Average Annual Growth Rate (%)	Contribution to Output Growth[a] (percentage points)
Labor input	68.6	0.58	0.40
Capital input	31.4	3.34	1.06
Plant	9.8	1.66	0.16
Equipment	14.1	4.67	0.66
Inventories	6.1	3.59	0.22
Land	1.4	1.76	0.02
Total input[b]	100.0		1.46
Manufacturing output		3.49	3.49
Total factor productivity			2.03[c]
Total factor productivity, based on BLS figures[d]			(1.97)

a. Column 1 (× .01) times column 2.
b. Total input = labor input + total capital input.
c. Total factor productivity growth = output growth minus total input growth.
d. Based on indexes of multifactor productivity, BLS Bulletin 2178, table 10, p. 24.

SOURCES: Weights: BLS Bulletin 2178, table 6, p. 20, and table C–29, p. 64. Growth rates reflect basic data from the following: Labor: indexes of hours of all persons, BLS Bulletin 2178, p. 24. Plant and equipment: gross stocks from Musgrave, "Fixed Capital Stocks in the United States," p. 59. Inventories: Bureau of Economic Analysis, *The National Income and Product Accounts of the United States, 1929–76*, pp. 223–26, table 5.11, line 6. Land: BLS Bulletin 2178, table C–28, p. 64. Output: BLS Bulletin 2178, table 10, p. 24.

The choice of weights in index numbers can be complex, but I have taken a simple approach and have used a midpoint for a span of years. Thus for changes in input over the period from 1948 to 1976 I use 1962 weights. For labor the weight is the share of employee compensation in gross product originating in manufacturing excluding a portion of indirect business taxes; the balance is allocated to capital.[23] Employee compensation, however, was adjusted to allow for the labor in proprietors' income and for the labor input of unpaid family workers; the capital share also reflects part of proprietors' income. Note in the weight column that labor earned almost 69 percent of the product and that the return to capital is divided among investments in plant, equipment, inventories, and land.[24] It is assumed, in accordance with conventional economic theory, that earnings of each type of capital are proportional to the value of the assets used.

For the change in inputs I have used recent Department of Labor estimates for labor. For capital input, the measurement of which involves many thorny issues, I did not attempt to duplicate newer approaches like those used by Jorgenson and the BLS but followed to some extent the treatment used by Denison and Kendrick in measuring the change of fixed capital input by the change in gross stocks in constant dollars as estimated by the Bureau of Economic Analysis (BEA).[25] BEA figures were also used for inventories. Growth rates for the various kinds of input are shown in the second column.

The third column shows the product of the first two columns, or the contribution to output growth. The weighted sum of inputs in the third column comes to 1.46 per year, which may be compared to an average growth rate of 3.49 percent for output. The difference of 2.03 percentage points per year between output and the weighted sum of inputs reflects the growth in total factor or multifactor productivity.

Among the inputs the contribution of labor, with a weight of 68.6 percent, accounted for 0.40 percentage points of output growth, reflecting the growth of employment (including that of proprietors and unpaid family workers) and the decline in the workweek of labor. Capital accounted for 1.06 percentage points of growth, of which fixed capital accounted for 0.82 points and inventories for most of the remaining 0.24 points.

From 1948 to 1976 the growth in the stock of capital in manufacturing not only was quite large but was accompanied by an increase in average weekly hours of capital, which constituted 11.9 percent of the growth in the stock (see table 2, last column). If the contribution of plant and equipment to output growth is increased by 11.9 percent, it is increased by 0.10 percentage points (0.82×0.119). This is my estimate of that part of the growth in total factor productivity in manufacturing from 1948 to 1976 that is attributable to a longer workweek for plant and equipment. The 0.10 percentage points are about 5 percent of the 2.0-point increase in the productivity of labor and capital combined and 2.8 percent of the 3.49-percentage-point rise in manufacturing output.

The last three columns of table 4 show the growth rate in total factor productivity for three post–World War II periods (each of about ten years' duration) and the importance of the longer workweek of capital. The middle period—1959 to 1969—was when the contribution of longer capital hours was greatest not only absolutely but also in relation to productivity growth, accounting for some 10 percent of the productivity rise. Longer capital hours accounted for some 30 percent of the acceleration in manufacturing productivity growth from 1948–1959 to 1959–1969 (0.20 − 0.06) ÷ (2.09 − 1.63) and almost 20 percent of the deceleration in productivity growth from 1959–1969 to 1969–1979. In spite of the temptation, I have purposely avoided a consideration of the role of capital hours in the extensively discussed productivity slowdown because of a lack of data. There is a strong suggestion, however, that my average capital hours effect and more conventional business cycle effects related to capacity utilization that I have omitted from my analysis would together constitute important components of the slowdown in manufacturing productivity growth.[26]

During the years from 1929 to 1948 the average growth of fixed capital in manufacturing was much smaller (only 1.0 percent per year)

TABLE 4

GROWTH RATE OF TOTAL FACTOR PRODUCTIVITY IN MANUFACTURING
AND EFFECT OF LONGER WORKWEEK OF CAPITAL, 1929–1979
(average percent per year)

	1929–48	1948–76	1948–59	1959–69	1969–79
Contribution of productivity rise to rise in manufacturing output	1.67	2.03	1.63	2.09	1.61
Effect of longer workweek of capital included in line above	0.07	0.10	0.06	0.20	0.11

SOURCES: For post–World War II years see text and tables 2 and 3. The 1929–1948 estimates are by the author, based mainly on Kendrick's data. Indexes of labor input and total output: Kendrick, *Productivity Trends*, p. 464. Gross capital stocks and inventories: BEA. Weights for 1929–1948 are from Kendrick, p. 453.

than it was from 1948 to 1976; so the estimated rise in the workweek of capital constituted a far greater proportion of the rise in the stock. Even so, the product of the plant and equipment contribution to growth (0.12 percentage points) and the capital hours adjustment (0.60) yields a smaller capital hours effect than from 1948 to 1976 (0.12 × 0.60 = 0.07). And since the average growth in total factor productivity in manufacturing was 1.67 percentage points over this period, the relative importance of the capital hours effect in productivity growth is somewhat smaller than it was in the postwar years—about 4 percent. Table 4 gives some summary figures, including a breakdown of the postwar period.

I extended the calculations to cover the entire private nonfarm business economy from 1948 to 1976 but excluded residential business from the nonfarm total because multiple shifts are not a relevant consideration with housing, which is used continuously (see table 5). A longer workweek of capital accounts for 0.056 percentage points of output growth for this sector. The 0.056 percentage points equal the contribution of plant and equipment to output growth as shown in the third column of the table—0.35 plus 0.73—times 5.2 percent from the last column of table 2. The 0.056 is almost 4 percent of the change in total factor productivity or about 1½ percent of the output change.

The changes cited above seem small on an overall basis, but they must be seen against the growth-accounting framework and in view of the fact that fixed-capital weights are not large. Furthermore, components of productivity change viewed in this fashion tend to be small, since we are talking about a total change of 1½ percent. Table 6 shows sources of multifactor productivity change for the private business economy from 1948 to 1981 according to recent BLS estimates of productivity.[27] These are the kinds of magnitudes with which my results should be compared.

If one accepts Denison's partitioning of productivity change, where would a rise in capital hours fit? There are three *major* components in Denison's productivity rise: (1) better resource allocation, as resources moved off farms into more productive nonfarm uses; (2) greater efficiencies due to the larger size of national, regional, and local markets and the economies associated with the increase in scale; (3) the increase in knowledge as a result of technological change, more skillful management, and so forth. Longer hours of capital could be related to all three components of productivity change. Assume, for example, that machinery manufacturers have developed a machine whose economical operation requires a three-shift day. This is an aspect of technological change, which is part of Denison's increase in knowledge. A longer workweek of capital could also be related to

TABLE 5

CONTRIBUTION TO THE GROWTH OF PRIVATE NONFARM BUSINESS
OUTPUT: LABOR INPUT, CAPITAL INPUT, AND TOTAL FACTOR
PRODUCTIVITY, 1948–1976

	1962 Weight (%)	Average Annual Growth Rate (%)	Contribution to Growth[a] (percentage points)
Labor input	65.0	1.14	0.74
Capital input	35.0	3.74[b]	1.31
Plant	12.7	2.74	0.35
Equipment	15.0	4.86	0.73
Inventories	3.8	3.75	0.14
Land	3.6	2.47	0.09
Total input[c]	100.0		2.05
Total output[d]		3.47	3.47
Total factor productivity[e]			1.42

a. Column 1 (× .01) times column 2.
b. Obtained implicitly by dividing column 3 by column 1.
c. Total input = labor input + total capital input.
d. Total output = real gross product of nonfarm business minus housing.
e. Total factor productivity = output growth minus total input growth.

SOURCES: Weights: BLS Bulletin 2178, table 6, p. 20, adjusted by author to exclude rental residential capital (table C–22), p. 62. Growth rates: Labor: indexes of hours of all persons in private nonfarm business, BLS Bulletin 2178, p. 23; Plant and equipment: BEA gross stocks in constant dollars for nonfarm business (Musgrave, "Fixed Capital Stocks in the United States," p. 59) less capital stock of nonprofit organizations (unpublished BEA data); Inventories: BEA, *The National Income and Product Accounts of the United States, 1929–76*, table 5.11, line 3, pp. 223–26; Land: indexes, BLS Bulletin 2178, table C–20, p. 62.

scale factors, which Denison assumes accounted for about 10 percent of productivity growth. Larger markets permit larger producing units; and, if these units entail more capital, they are likely to work longer hours. Finally, the shift of resources from farms may have been facilitated by the construction of factories in outlying areas where factories could be operated two or more shifts.

Although Denison's is a powerful framework that has greatly expanded our understanding of growth, I am by no means sure that the preceding discussion in growth-accounting terms is the best way to view the importance of a phenomenon like a longer workweek of capital. The fundamental question is whether the increase in the stock of capital that occurred in the post–World War II period would have

TABLE 6

SOURCES OF MULTIFACTOR PRODUCTIVITY CHANGE IN PRIVATE BUSINESS, 1948–1981

Source of Productivity Change	Change (percentage points)	Distribution (%)
Shifts of labor off farms	0.1	7
Changes in composition of labor force[a]	0.4	27
Research and development	0.2	13
Hours worked in lieu of hours paid	−0.1	−7
Total of above factors	0.6	40
Unexplained	0.9	60
Total multifactor productivity	1.5	100

a. Chiefly education.
SOURCE: BLS Bulletin 2178, p. 31.

been as great had possibilities not existed for increased shift work in noncontinuous industries. It is well known that over the postwar period (and before that also) there has been a major substitution of capital for labor. This change has occurred for two main reasons. First, I believe that the trend of technological change in manufacturing has been chiefly capital using and labor saving. Second, the price of labor has gone up more rapidly than the price of capital.[28] One of the factors reducing the price of capital has been the potential for shift work. This in turn has fostered the rise of more capital-intensive methods of production than would otherwise have been the case.[29]

The past few years have highlighted the difficulties of many firms and entire industries that were once the bulwark of U.S. manufacturing. Firms and industries can stagnate. But some manage to adapt to new competitive environments, and these are the firms and industries that are the growing part of the economy. That shift work was adopted on a broad scale in the United States in the postwar period suggests that it must have been important at the margin in the location of new plants and in the mobility of capital generally. The movement of capital to the South—not to mention to foreign countries— probably occurred not only because wages were lower in the South but also because business had opportunities to operate capital more efficiently than was possible on a single-shift basis. The same might be said about the movement of factories out of cities to nonmetropolitan areas since the mid-1960s, as the data in table 22 suggest. This is not to deny the importance of other factors, such as access to raw materials and markets, tax considerations, and transportation costs, in the location decision.

To demonstrate the importance of the growth of shift work in this context would require a model in which the growth of shift work, on the one hand, would be an aspect of increased capital input and, on the other hand, would be an influence affecting capital costs, like the cost of plant and equipment, depreciation rates, interest rates, taxes, and maintenance costs. Such an attempt, however, is beyond the scope of the study.

The Longer Workweek of Capital and the Long-Run Rise in Utilization

In my earliest study of equipment utilization in manufacturing, I found (using data on electric-power consumption and horsepower of electric motors) that an average unit of equipment worked 31.4 percent more hours per year in 1954 than in 1929.[30] I can now answer at least tentatively the question I could only speculate about when I wrote that article, namely, How much of this rise is attributable to a lengthening in the workweek of capital—as a result of more shift work—and how much is due to more efficient use of capital by management? At that time I felt that both influences were relevant.

The figures below in the left-hand column for 1929, 1939, and 1954 are indexes of annual hours worked by capital equipment in manufacturing from my early study. They have been supplemented with my estimate for 1963 because since that article was published in June 1963, the Bureau of the Census collected figures on electric power consumption in the 1963 Annual Survey of Manufactures and on horsepower of electric motors at the end of 1962 in the 1963 Census of Manufactures. I constructed the 1963 index on a basis comparable with that for the earlier years.[31]

	Original	Revised
1929	100.0	100.0
1939	95.6	*
1954	131.4	128.3
1963	147.7	148.7

* Not calculated.

These are the only years shown because they are the only ones for which census data exist. These are overall indexes of hours operated per year per unit of equipment—utilization rates—with which we can compare the changes in the workweek of manufacturing capital from the present study. Before making this comparison, however, I was able to improve on some of my original estimates. I was able to calculate 1929 equipment utilization rates by industry—as distinct from a rate for manufacturing as a whole—because I was able to obtain electric power consumption data not previously available by industry. I calculated the change in these industry utilization rates from 1929 to 1954, weighting the detailed changes together by fixed weights to derive a figure for all of manufacturing. The use of fixed weights has the effect of reducing the influence of changes in industry mix. (See note 21 for an illustration of the general principle.) I used a similar procedure to calculate the change in equipment utilization in manufacturing from 1954 to 1963.[32] These are the revised figures shown in the right-hand column above. A comparison of the old and new indexes in 1954 and 1963 does not point to large mix effects.

Table 7 summarizes the findings in terms of annual rates of growth. The first column gives the change in annual hours worked per unit of equipment for all reasons, or the change in overall utilization rates. The second column gives the change in hours due to a longer workweek of capital—essentially, increased shift work.

Over the thirty-four years from 1929 to 1963 the increase in the workweek of capital was 39 percent of the overall rise in annual hours worked by capital equipment in manufacturing. Thus all other factors taken as a group were more important than the longer workweek of capital.[33] According to the table (third column) the ratio was greater than the 1929–1976 average from 1929 to 1954 but much less than average from 1954 to 1963. The years 1954 and 1963 are not good terminal years for the analysis of growth in relation to 1929 because

---

TABLE 7

ANNUAL RATES OF CHANGE IN HOURS WORKED BY CAPITAL
EQUIPMENT IN MANUFACTURING, BY SOURCE, 1929–1963

	All Sources	Longer Workweek of Capital	Ratio of Longer Workweek of Capital to All Sources[a]
1929–1963	1.17	0.46	0.39
1929–1954	1.00	0.51	0.51
1954–1963	1.65	0.35	0.21

a. Column 2 ÷ column 1.
SOURCES: Column 1: indexes shown in text. Column 2: based on indexes in manufacturing, table 1.

they are either recession or early recovery years. With some rough adjustments I made estimates for 1955 and 1964, which are years of high employment. For the thirty-five years from 1929 to 1964 the ratio (third column) would be unchanged, but for the two subperiods, 1929–1955 and 1955–1964, the ratios would be almost equal.

Going beyond 1963 is risky because it is probably pushing the data too far. There are no horsepower figures beyond 1962; we must rely instead on aggregate gross stocks of equipment measured in constant dollars. Certain ratios intrinsic to the estimates of electric power use come from a 1945 survey by the Federal Power Commission, which may no longer be valid. If we do take the leap, however, the year 1973 is a good stopping point because the great price increases caused by the Arab oil embargo set off a wave of economizing on energy use throughout the economy.

For our purposes, electric power use in manufacturing rose 64.1 percent from 1963 to 1973. Real gross stocks of equipment rose 58.3 percent according to estimates by the BEA, which implies an increase in annual hours per unit of equipment of 3.7 percent, or 0.36 percent per year. Since the workweek of capital rose at an annual rate of 0.52 percent, other influences must have partly offset this rise attributable to a longer workweek of capital. What these other influences might be is hard to say since they can originate in so many different ways. In any case, answers to these questions belong to a different investigation. Here we might take note of some new thinking about capital utilization and idleness, which stresses that maximizing weekly or annual hours per unit of capital equipment may not necessarily be optimal when all factors of production are taken into account.[34]

Implications

Economic policy of the present administration rests in part on the propositions that this country does not save enough of its income and that the main reasons for our low private saving are the disincentives caused by high taxation. More saving will mean more private investment in plant and equipment and ultimately a more vigorous growth in productivity.[35] Our saving rate appears somewhat low compared with those of other major countries. It is a big leap, however, from gross saving rates to productivity levels or productivity growth. The main point of this study has been that hours worked by capital in the United States have lengthened. Some years ago Denison pointed out that in the 1950s shift work was more common in the United States than in other major industrialized countries. The level and growth of shift work and the efficiency with which capital is used are of some importance in making meaningful comparisons of saving and invest-ment among nations. Countries that use their capital more intensively require less gross saving on that account.

In this regard it is interesting that some countries have attempted through legislation to place restrictions on night work because of its undesirable effects on the health of workers. That I have not at-tempted to discuss health, psychological, social, and other issues in this study does not mean that noneconomic arguments against night work are without merit. A society may choose to limit night work if such limitation is considered desirable; however, the economic conse-quences should be understood. Outright prohibitions or limitations of this kind would reduce productivity that takes the form of economiz-ing on the use of capital. Furthermore, insofar as technological change continues to be capital using and labor saving, a prohibition or limita-tion of such work could have negative consequences for productivity growth. In the long run such a limitation would lead to larger plants operating a single shift, with possibly some offsets due to larger size.

Prohibitions against shift work would be a kind of throwback to legislation that appeared in the nineteenth century limiting night work. The early legislation was concerned with the health and welfare of women and children, which seem not to be issues at present. Today in this country organized labor is much more accepting of shift work, recognizing the benefits that accrue through more efficient use of capital while pointing out the drawbacks it sees.[36] In fact, during the recession we could observe many union contracts being reopened to reconsider not merely scheduled wage and benefit increases but also "work rules," which often have an important effect on productivity.

In the past, capital has been substituted for labor insofar as labor costs have risen more rapidly than capital costs. Capital costs embrace the costs of operating capital, the most important of which (aside from labor) is the cost of energy. The rise in energy costs since 1973 has been so great that all energy users have been engaged in massive efforts aimed at conservation.[37] To the extent that business uses less capital-intensive methods, shift work will be discouraged, but the extent to which this kind of substitution may have occurred is still obscure. We do know that business has made major reductions in energy use per unit of output, but we do not know the composition of this change. That is, reduced energy per unit of output may come about because of reduced energy per unit of capital or less capital per unit of output or both, with the mix of output held constant.

"Time-of-day" pricing by electric utilities is an innovation that could foster shift work.[38] Some utilities (Wisconsin seems to provide the leading example) have set up rate schedules that offer lower rates for off-peak hours. If the reduction in rates is sufficiently large, it might offset the premiums that have to be paid to labor for night work. Industries that are now capital intensive, however, are probably already working night shifts. What might limit a movement to shift work from this source is that energy costs for *all* purposes are far smaller than labor costs, so that the nighttime energy discount would have to be very large. Of course, falling energy costs such as occurred in 1982 and 1983 will work in the opposite direction from what has just been described.

The future of shift work will depend on the same basic forces that have always operated. Whether the trend of technological change will continue to be capital using and labor saving remains to be seen. The development of minicomputers suggests that technological change is not always in the same direction. Robots are an innovation very much in the news. The development of robots could bring about a longer workweek for capital; at the moment capital represented by robots is very small, in this country at least. The possibilities of Saturday and Sunday factory operations even for one-shift plants would be greatly extended since, except for the supervision of robots, factories would not have to pay the time-and-a-half premium for overtime wages. Moreover, firms that now operate a single shift might find late-shift work economical, and firms that now operate two shifts might find three shifts economical. So far as added shifts are concerned, the saving in labor costs would be smaller for second-shift operations than for equivalent time on Saturday and Sunday operations because the shift differential is not large in the United States. Third-shift operations could expand relatively more than second insofar as working the third shift (say, midnight to eight in the morning) may be limited at present by difficulties in recruiting labor in noncontinuous industries generally. Conceivably, use of robots coupled with low energy rates at night would cause firms that now work one shift to switch operations from daytime to nighttime, although that in itself would not increase the average workweek of capital.

Finding out more about how capital is used should enhance our understanding of productivity growth in this country. From 1929 to 1963 the apparent increase in the utilization of equipment in manufacturing in the form of longer hours per year per unit of equipment was due more to better management than to increased weekly hours attributable to additional shift work. Apparently management improvements that raise the hours per year worked by machinery do not grow at a constant rate, as my very tentative findings for 1963–1973 seem to suggest. Beyond this many questions remain unanswered. Has the trend toward a reduction in idle machinery time been optimal with respect to total costs? Are factory work-in-process inventories "excessive," as has been suggested, offsetting some of the economies that have come from more intensive use of plant and equipment?[39] These are some of the questions that may be answered by greater research efforts in the area of capital utilization.

Notes

1. The literature on this subject is very large. For early studies see, for example, Moses Abramovitz, *Resource and Output Trends in the United States since 1870*, National Bureau of Economic Research Occasional Paper no. 42 (New York, 1956); Edward F. Denison, *The Sources of Economic Growth in the United States and the Alternatives before Us*, Committee for Economic Development Supplementary Paper no. 13 (New York, 1962); Solomon Fabricant, *Basic Facts on Productivity Change*, National Bureau of Economic Research Occasional Paper no. 63 (New York, 1959); John W. Kendrick, *Productivity Trends in the United States* (Princeton, N.J.: Princeton University Press for National Bureau of Economic Research, 1961); and Robert M. Solow, "Technical Change and the Aggregate Production Function," *Review of Economics and Statistics* (August 1957), pp. 312-20.

For more recent works see Martin Neil Baily, "Productivity and the Services of Capital and Labor," *Brookings Papers on Economic Activity (BPEA)*, no. 1 (1981), pp. 1-50, and "The Productivity Growth Slowdown by Industry," *BPEA*, no. 2 (1982), pp. 423-60; U.S. Department of Labor, Bureau of Labor Statistics, *Trends in Multifactor Productivity, 1948-81*, Bulletin 2178 (September 1983) (hereafter BLS Bulletin 2178); Peter Clark, "Investment in the 1970's: Theory, Performance and Production," *BPEA*, no. 1 (1979), pp. 73-113, and "Issues in the Analysis of Capital Formation and Productivity Growth," *BPEA*, no. 2 (1979), pp. 423-31; Edward F. Denison, *Accounting for United States Economic Growth, 1929-1969* (Washington, D.C.: Brookings Institution, 1974), *Accounting for Slower Economic Growth: The United States in the 1970s* (Washington, D.C.: Brookings Institution, 1979), and "Accounting for Slower Economic Growth: An Update," in John W. Kendrick, ed., *International Comparisons of Productivity and Causes of the Slowdown* (Cambridge, Mass.: Ballinger, forthcoming); Barbara M. Fraumeni and Dale W. Jorgenson, "The Role of Capital in U.S. Economic Growth, 1948-1976," in George M. von Furstenberg, ed., *Capital, Efficiency and Growth* (Cambridge, Mass.: Ballinger Publishing Co., 1980), pp. 9-250; Dale W. Jorgenson, "Accounting for Capital," in von Furstenberg, *Capital, Efficiency and Growth*, pp. 251-319; John W. Kendrick and Elliott S. Grossman, *Productivity in the United States* (Baltimore, Md.: Johns Hopkins University Press, 1980); J. R. Norsworthy and L. J. Fulco, "Productivity and Costs in the Private Economy," *Monthly Labor Review* (September 1976); J. R. Norsworthy and M. J. Harper, *The Role of Capital Formation in the Recent Productivity Slowdown*, BLS Working Paper no. 87 (1979); and J. R. Norsworthy, M. J. Harper, and Kent Kunze, "The Slowdown in Productivity Growth: Analysis of Some Contributing Factors," *BPEA*, no. 2 (1979), pp. 387-431.

2. BLS Bulletin 2178, pp. 73–80.

3. For industry studies see, for example, Kendrick, *Productivity Trends;* Frank M. Gollop and Dale W. Jorgenson, "U.S. Productivity Growth by Industry, 1947–73," in John W. Kendrick and Beatrice N. Vaccara, eds., *New Developments in Productivity Measurement and Analysis,* Studies in Income and Wealth, vol. 44 (Chicago: University of Chicago Press for National Bureau of Economic Research, 1980), pp. 17–136; Fraumeni and Jorgenson, "The Role of Capital in U.S. Economic Growth," pp. 9–250; and J. R. Norsworthy and M. J. Harper, "Productivity Growth in Manufacturing in the 1980's: Labor, Capital and Energy," in American Statistical Association, *Proceedings of the Business and Economics Section* (1979), pp. 17–26.

4. For studies covering earlier time periods see Abramovitz, *Resource and Output Trends;* Denison, *Sources of Economic Growth;* Fabricant, *Basic Facts on Productivity Change;* and Kendrick, *Productivity Trends.*

5. For a recent study, see Edward F. Denison, "The Contribution of Capital to Economic Growth," *American Economic Review,* vol. 70, no. 2 (May 1980), pp. 220–24.

6. For an early study see Dale W. Jorgenson and Zvi Griliches, "The Explanation of Productivity Change," *Review of Economic Studies,* vol. 34 (July 1967), pp. 249–83, reprinted in *Survey of Current Business: The Measurement of Productivity,* vol. 52, no. 5 (May 1972), pp. 3–36. For a recent study see BLS Bulletin 2178, Appendixes C and F.

7. Moses Abramovitz, "Resource and Output Trends in the United States since 1870," *American Economic Review: Papers and Proceedings* (1956), p. 11.

8. BLS Bulletin 2178, p. 31.

9. Denison has also measured the influence of lesser factors, such as pollution controls, worker-safety and health regulations, crime, and labor disputes, among others. See his *Accounting for Slower Economic Growth,* chap. 7.

10. Nestor E. Terleckyj, "Sources of Productivity Advance: A Pilot Study of Manufacturing Industries, 1899–1953" (Ph.D. diss., Columbia University, 1960); *Effects of R & D on the Productivity Growth of Industries* (Washington, D.C.: National Planning Association, 1974); and "What Do R & D Numbers Tell Us about Technological Change?" *American Economic Review: Papers and Proceedings,* vol. 70, no. 2 (May 1980), pp. 55–61; and John W. Kendrick, *Postwar Productivity Trends in the United States, 1948–1969* (New York: National Bureau of Economic Research, 1973), pp. 134–43.

11. Richard R. Nelson and Sidney Winter, "In Search of a Useful Theory of Innovation," *Research Policy,* vol. 6 (Summer 1977), pp. 36–76.

12. Edwin Mansfield, "Research and Development, Productivity Change and Public Policy," in *Relationships between R & D and Economic Growth/Productivity* (Washington, D.C.: National Science Foundation, November 9, 1977); Zvi Griliches, "Research Expenditures and Growth Accounting," in B. R. Williams, ed., *Science and Technology in Economic Growth* (New York: John Wiley, 1973), pp. 59–95, and "Returns to Research and Development in the Private Sector," in Kendrick and Vaccara, *New Developments in Productivity Measurement and Analysis,* pp. 419–61.

13. National Research Council, *Measurement and Interpretation of Productivity*

(Washington, D.C.: National Academy of Sciences, 1979), p. 163.

14. Theodore W. Schultz, "A Comment on Education and Economic Growth," in Kendrick, *International Comparisons of Productivity and Causes of the Slowdown.*

15. Richard R. Nelson, "Research on Productivity Growth and Productivity Differences," *Journal of Economic Literature,* vol. 19 (September 1981), p. 1035. This article is a good summary of the state of productivity research.

16. A capacity utilization variable seemed to have no explanatory power in some regressions I ran for the year 1976. See Murray F. Foss, *Changes in the Workweek of Fixed Capital: U.S. Manufacturing, 1929 to 1976* (Washington, D.C.: American Enterprise Institute, 1981), pp. 45–46.

17. Robin Marris, *The Economics of Capital Utilization* (Cambridge: Cambridge University Press, 1964); Gordon C. Winston, "Capital Utilization in Economic Development," *Economic Journal,* vol. 81, no. 321 (March 1971), pp. 36–60; and Roger R. Betancourt and Christopher K. Clague, *Capital Utilization: A Theoretical and Empirical Analysis* (New York: Cambridge University Press, 1981). Earlier works by Betancourt and Clague and by Winston appear in Foss, *Changes in the Workweek of Fixed Capital,* pp. 99–104.

18. Murray F. Foss, "The Utilization of Capital Equipment," *Survey of Current Business,* vol. 43 (June 1963), pp. 8–16.

19. Edward F. Denison clarified this distinction in a growth-accounting context in what I have called the "capital utilization controversy." A brief summary of this controversy appeared in Foss, *Changes in the Workweek of Fixed Capital,* pp. 4–7. Major papers by Denison, on the one hand, and Griliches and Jorgenson, on the other, appear in *Survey of Current Business: The Measurement of Productivity,* vol. 52, no. 5 (May 1972).

20. In this connection several investigators have noted the role of indivisibilities. For example, Kuznets emphasized the buildup of infrastructure in the early phases of industrial development, that is, the construction of utilities, railroad lines, and so forth, in explaining why the share of construction in relation to equipment declined over the long run. Simon Kuznets, *Capital in the American Economy: Its Formation and Financing* (Princeton, N.J.: Princeton University Press for the National Bureau of Economic Research, 1961), pp. 142–73. See also James M. Malcomson, "Capacity Utilization, the User Cost of Capital and the Cost of Adjustment," *International Economic Review,* vol. 16, pp. 352–61.

21. Suppose there were two industries, one of which always worked its capital around the clock whereas the other always worked forty hours a week. If the capital stock of the former industry grew more rapidly than that of the latter, the average workweek of the combined stock would show a rise if weights were permitted to vary.

22. See references in note 1 and, as an example, Denison, *Accounting for United States Economic Growth,* chap. 8.

23. See the notes to table 3 for specific sources.

24. The average labor share in manufacturing from 1948 to 1976 was 69.0 percent according to the latest BLS study. See BLS Bulletin 2178, table 6, p. 20.

25. Kendrick used a gross measure for fixed capital inputs in his latest

study. Denison used a combination of gross and net with the former weighted by three and the latter by one. In manufacturing, changes in gross and net stocks as estimated by the BEA from 1948 to 1973 are fairly similar. See Denison, *Accounting for United States Economic Growth*, pp. 52–56. For a discussion of some of the issues in the newer approaches to measuring capital input, see BLS Bulletin 2178, pp. 39–65, especially the reference in footnote 1, p. 40.

I have introduced an inconsistency in combining BLS weights with my rates of change for capital inputs, but the differences between my results and a consistent set of figures are probably very small.

26. Capacity utilization effects alone are thought to be important. See BLS Bulletin 2178, p. 28, including notes.

27. Ibid., p. 31.

28. This has been pointed out in many studies. The BLS shows a 3 percent per annum decline in the price of capital services in relation to that of labor in the private business sector, 1948–1981. Ibid., p. 21.

29. This point is given considerable stress by Betancourt and Clague, *Capital Utilization*, p. 5 especially.

30. Foss, "Utilization of Capital Equipment."

31. A minor adjustment had to be made because the horsepower figures had to be estimated for the end, rather than the beginning, of 1963. See ibid.

32. The 1929–1954 changes by industry were weighted by an average of the 1929 relative proportion of horsepower by industry and the 1954 relative proportion. The 1954–1963 changes were weighted by an average of the 1954 and the 1962 relative proportions.

33. In the "utilization controversy" Denison put considerable stress on "management improvements" as a reason for the increased utilization of capital. Denison, "Some Major Issues in Productivity Analysis," in *Survey of Current Business: The Measurement of Productivity*, vol. 52, no. 5, part 2, p. 57. In this respect the findings in this study support the general position taken by Denison in this controversy.

34. See Gordon Winston, *The Timing of Economic Activities: Firms, Households and Markets, and Time-Specific Analysis* (New York: Cambridge University Press, 1982), and Walter Y. Oi, "Slack Capacity: Productive or Wasteful?" *American Economic Review*, vol. 71, no. 2 (May 1981), pp. 64–69. See also Steven J. Marcus, "Making Tasks in Factory Fit," *New York Times*, September 15, 1983, sec. D.

35. I am ignoring—but not because they are unimportant—the large actual and prospective federal budget deficits that have been widely discussed since 1981 and that will reduce the supply of saving available for total investment.

36. See John Zalusky, "Shift Work—A Complex of Problems," *AFL–CIO Federationist*, vol. 85, pp. 1–6.

37. In a recent paper Dale Jorgenson argued that the huge rise in energy costs since 1973 was the main reason for the slowdown in the growth of productivity. Dale W. Jorgenson, "The Role of Energy in the Productivity Slowdown," in Kendrick, *International Comparisons of Productivity and Causes of the Slowdown*. Ernst R. Berndt, the discussant, expressed considerable sympathy for the Jorgenson analysis but felt that the effect of high energy costs on

capital-labor substitution was of a long-run nature and could not have had much of an effect on the productivity slowdown from 1973 to date.

38. Joann S. Lublin, "Blues in the Night," *Wall Street Journal*, October 18, 1977; also Lawrence Rout, "Environmentalists Are Split over Issue of Time-of-Day Pricing of Electricity," *Wall Street Journal*, October 15, 1978.

39. See Marcus, "Making Tasks in Factory Fit," and Robert H. Hayes, "Why Japanese Factories Work," *Harvard Business Review* (July–August 1981), pp. 57–66.

2

Estimating Average Weekly Plant Hours in Manufacturing for the Period between 1929 and 1976

In this study the points of departure for manufacturing are the changes in average weekly plant hours derived in the first study and summarized in tables 8 and 9.[1] Table 8 gives overall results for all manufacturing using different kinds of weights, and table 9 gives the breakdown by two-digit manufacturing industries. I decided to use the overall change of 24.7 percent from 1929 to 1976 as my controlling total for manufacturing (see table 8, line C). This figure omits a possible adjustment of 4.5 percent that would allow for the fact that 1976 weekly plant hours were probably low in relation to those of 1929. On the average, 1929 was a year of high activity whereas 1976 represented an early phase of the cyclical recovery from the recession that reached bottom in April 1975.[2] Our problem is to estimate the path of average weekly plant hours between the two terminal or benchmark years.

Department of Labor Sources of Data

There are two main sources of data for interpolating between 1929 and 1976. Neither source measures directly what is presented in tables 8 and 9, but each is useful for our purposes. The data, from the Bureau of Labor Statistics (BLS), refer to the proportion of production workers actually employed on late shifts. I use changes in these proportions as interpolators of average weekly plant hours; the exact procedure is described in some detail in this chapter.

For many years in its Industry Wage Survey series the BLS has conducted surveys of wages and conditions of employment.[3] These surveys usually show, among other things, data on the proportion of production workers employed on late shifts. When I started this work I had thought it would be possible to obtain information for a sample of industries starting with recent years and going back into the 1920s, but shift information was mentioned only infrequently in surveys

TABLE 8

ALTERNATIVE MEASURES OF AVERAGE WEEKLY PLANT HOURS IN MANUFACTURING AND THEIR CHANGE, 1929–1976

Variant	1929	1976	Change (%)
A[a]	66.5	81.8	23.0
B[b]	91.9	110.3	20.0
C[c]	—	—	24.7

a. Hours for each detailed and major industry weighted by employment in each year.
b. Capital weighted throughout. 1976: gross fixed assets at detailed (four-digit) level used to obtain average weekly plant hours for each major (two-digit) level and to obtain average weekly plant hours for all manufacturing. 1929: same as 1976 except that horsepower is used to combine detailed and major industry groups.
c. Percentage change in capital-weighted average weekly plant hours for each major industry weighted by gross fixed capital stocks in 1972 prices for 1954 as estimated by Bureau of Labor Statistics.

SOURCES: Variant A, U.S. Department of Commerce, Bureau of the Census, *Survey of Plant Capacity*, M2–C (1976), table 1. All other statistics are estimates by author on the basis of data from Census Bureau.

conducted by the BLS before World War II. Ordinarily the BLS did not summarize these surveys; in any case, the most one could get from them would be series for particular industries taken a few times at seemingly irregular intervals.

The BLS also instituted a series of wage studies covering individual metropolitan areas starting sometime in the early 1950s.[4] In addition to showing individual area data, starting around 1959 the BLS began to present national averages for all metropolitan areas combined and for four regions.[5] These studies have the virtue of constituting time series; however, they provide no industry breakdowns, and the aggregated figures are mixtures of different time periods because most individual metropolitan areas were surveyed by the BLS only once every three years. When the BLS published a national or regional average for all metropolitan areas, the average was a composite of figures for the current year for some areas, for the previous year for other areas, and for the previous two years for the remaining areas. Depending on the employment weights, the averages would thus reflect a lag of one and a fraction years. It is possible to make use of the disaggregated data, however, and information of this sort plays a major role in the estimates presented here.[6]

Table 10 presents the national averages of the proportion of manufacturing production workers actually employed on late shifts for all

TABLE 9

AVERAGE WEEKLY PLANT HOURS AND THEIR CHANGE, BY MAJOR INDUSTRY, 1929–1976

Industry	1929	1976	Change (%)
Food	88.0	90.3	2.6
Tobacco	49.2	104.4	112.2
Textiles	66.8	115.6	73.0
Apparel	46.0	46.3	0.6
Lumber	58.2	62.6	7.6
Furniture	50.3	52.6	4.6
Paper	128.7	139.6	8.5
Printing and publishing	62.7	82.8	32.0
Chemicals	108.1	138.2	27.8
Petroleum	157.8	162.9	3.2
Rubber	103.7	120.0	15.7
Leather	49.4	45.6	−7.7
Stone, clay, and glass	104.6	119.3	14.1
Primary metals	125.5	142.4	13.5
Fabricated metals	55.6	77.8	39.9
Machinery	55.7	83.5	49.9
Electrical machinery	49.6	77.0	55.2
Transportation equipment	60.5	88.8	46.8
Instruments	59.5	76.6	28.7
Miscellaneous	49.3	62.1	26.0

SOURCE: Estimates by author based on data from Census Bureau. Reflects use of capital weights.

metropolitan areas as well as breakdowns for the four regions. The national average shows a fairly steady rise to 1974–1975; then it shows a dip and a partial recovery. What the BLS published as the 1974–1975 average in fact reflects patterns that center on 1973 and the first half of 1974.

A breakdown by region shows small upward trends in the Northeast and in the South and a strong upward trend in the North Central region. The latter may have been the result of the Vietnam War and some fundamental changes in the methods of production in the North Central states. But equally interesting is the West, which peaked in 1967–1968 and then fell back to where it had been at the start of the 1960s. This decline may have been a reflection of the slowdown in the space program and cutbacks in defense and electronics. In any case these movements suggest the presence of long-lasting influences—

TABLE 10

PERCENTAGE OF PRODUCTION WORKERS ON LATE SHIFTS IN MANUFACTURING, ALL METROPOLITAN AREAS, 1959–1980

Period	United States	Northeast	South	North Central	West
1959–1960	22.8[a]				
1960–1961	22.2	19.6	24.4	23.5	22.8
1961–1962	21.5	19.5	24.9	22.0	21.2
1962–1963	23.2	20.5	25.6	24.5	23.1
1963–1964	23.3	21.0	24.9	25.5	22.6
1964–1965	24.3	21.5	24.9	26.7	23.4
1965–1966	25.0	22.4	25.5	27.4	24.3
1966–1967	25.8	22.4	26.2	25.4	25.2
1967–1968	26.0	22.6	25.9	28.8	25.8
1968–1969[b]	26.1	22.6	26.0	29.2	25.4
1969–1970	26.2	22.7	26.1	29.5	25.1
1970–1971	26.6	22.5	26.1	31.1	23.4
1971–1972	26.3	22.8	26.3	30.4	22.3
1971–1973	27.9	23.4	27.2	33.3	22.1
1972–1974	27.7	23.7	27.3	32.4	23.4
1975	28.9	23.2	26.7	36.6	22.2
1976	26.8	22.2	27.3	31.6	22.2
1977	26.9	22.0	27.3	31.8	22.5
1978	27.8	24.0	27.8	32.5	23.3
1979	28.4	24.6	27.9	33.6	23.2
1980	28.1	24.4	28.2	33.0	22.5

a. Appears in Charles M. O'Connor, "Late-Shift Employment in Manufacturing Industries," *Monthly Labor Review* (November 1970), p. 37.
b. Summary not available. Straight-line interpolations for United States and each region after examining detailed area results.
SOURCES: BLS Area Wage Survey Summaries. Specific summary reports from 1960–1961 to 1973–1974 are listed in BLS, *Directory of Occupational Wage Surveys*, p. 6. For 1975, 1976, and 1977 see BLS Bulletins 1850–89, 1900–82, and 1950–77. Data for the latest years were supplied directly by the BLS.

possibly a long business cycle ordinarily difficult to observe in the data. Linear trends were fitted to the table 10 data for the United States and three of the regions and are shown in table 11.

Detailed Procedure

The main problems with these aggregated metropolitan area figures are their somewhat limited scope—only twenty-one years for the U.S.

35

TABLE 11

EQUATIONS RELATING PROPORTIONS OF PRODUCTION WORKERS
ON LATE SHIFTS IN MANUFACTURING TO TIME, UNITED STATES
AND THREE REGIONS, 1959–1980

	Constant	Coefficient on Time	t-Statistics	$\bar{r}^2$
United States[a]	18.1	0.32	7.6	.84
United States[b]	18.0	0.32	9.5	.82
Northeast[b]	17.4	0.20	7.0	.72
South[b]	21.9	0.18	15.0	.92
North Central[b]	14.7	0.60	9.2	.81

a. 1959–1960 to 1980: twenty-one observations.
b. 1960–1961 to 1980: twenty observations.
SOURCE: Calculations by author. Basic data: table 10.

totals—and ambiguous dating. If one focused on the individual area reports that lie behind the regional and national averages, however, one could extend the period back to the early 1950s and could be precise about the timing. Consequently I have turned to time series for individual metropolitan areas, for many of which the series proved to be quite long.

An examination of figures for several dozen individual areas revealed that the proportion of workers on late shifts was often subject to rather pronounced cyclical fluctuations. I interpreted these fluctuations to be a consequence chiefly of the changing industrial mix of employment. For example, steel is a three-shift industry whereas meatpacking is mainly (but not exclusively) one shift. When durable goods output falls in a recession, employment in steel falls in relation to employment in meatpacking; so the overall proportion of workers on late shifts will fall for the whole metropolitan area. A reversal occurs with the recovery, but mix effects of this kind are not what is wanted for this study. Although I did fit time trends to each of several dozen metropolitan areas, in the end I decided that the best procedure would be to analyze proportions of workers on late shifts at business cycle peaks.

For each of forty-nine metropolitan areas I determined by inspection the peak proportion around 1960 (usually 1959), around 1970 (usually 1969), and around 1978–1979. To get averages for all areas combined at each peak I weighted each metropolitan proportion by a set of fixed weights, namely, value added in manufacturing in the

TABLE 12

Manufacturing Production Workers on Late Shifts,
from Two Studies, 1952–1979
(percent)

Period	This Study	United States Metropolitan Area (average)
1952	21.9	n.a.
1959–1960	22.3	22.8
1969	25.8	26.2
1978–1979	28.2	28.1

n.a. = not available.
Sources: Column 1: see text. Column 2: BLS; see table 10.

metropolitan area in 1967. I wanted fixed weights since my 1929–1976 change in average weekly plant hours for all manufacturing employed fixed weights (1954 real gross fixed assets). The year 1967 was simply a midpoint for years I was able to measure with these metropolitan data (1959–1979). And value added is a better measure for combining areas than employment, although some capital measure—which was not available—would have been better still. On the basis of a smaller number of areas, the data were extended back to 1952. Results of this procedure are shown in table 12. The average annual arithmetic increase of 0.31 percentage points from 1959–1960 to 1978–1979 is virtually the same as the coefficient on time shown in table 10: 0.32 percentage points. These percentages in the first column of table 12 should be viewed as points on a high-employment trend line, but they are just the starting point for our estimating procedure described below.

The all-manufacturing figures just cited reflect a broad range of industries—those, like apparel, that rarely if ever employ shift work and those, like petroleum refining, that operate around the clock through shift work. To see better the growth in late-shift work, it is useful to exclude these two groups from the total so we are left with industries where *some* shift work has been employed. The calculations are shown in table 13. The first line under each year in table 13 shows total production worker employment for all manufacturing from the BLS establishment estimates. Column 1 is multiplied by the proportions (column 2) taken from table 12 (with an additional decimal point) to yield production workers working late shifts (column 3) and, after subtraction, workers *not* working late shifts (column 4). I have

TABLE 13

Production Workers Employed on Late and Daytime Shifts in Manufacturing, by Shift Status of Industry, 1952–1979

Shift Status of Industry	Total (millions) (1)	Percentage on Late Shifts (2)	Number on Late Shifts (millions) (3)	Number Not on Late Shifts (daytime) (millions) (4)
1952				
Total	13.36	21.92	2.93	10.43
No-shift	1.72	0.00	0.00	1.72
Continuous	1.32	42.60	0.56	0.76
All-other	10.32	22.96	2.37	7.95
1959–1960				
Total	12.59	22.32	2.81	9.78
No-shift	1.73	0.00	0.00	1.73
Continuous	1.18	42.40	0.50	0.68
All-other	9.69	23.84	2.31	7.37

1969				
Total	14.77	25.84	3.82	10.95
No-shift	1.92	0.00	0.00	1.92
Continuous	1.23	42.40	0.52	0.71
All-other	11.62	28.40	3.30	8.32
1978–1979				
Total	14.90	28.21	4.20	10.70
No-shift	1.75	0.00	0.00	1.75
Continuous	1.16	41.90	0.48	0.65
All-other	11.99	31.03	3.72	8.27

SOURCE: See text.

39

applied a proportion taken from an aggregation of metropolitan areas to a national employment total. Metropolitan areas account for some 80 percent of national establishment employment in manufacturing. Whether the *trend* in these percentages is correct is another matter; and, because it is of some importance, it is discussed below.

The second line under each year shows no-shift industries. Initially I thought I would trace employment of detailed industries that worked less than ten hours per day in 1976; but since this proved difficult, I decided to use as a proxy production worker employment in apparel, furniture, and leather, taking the entire two-digit total for each. These three groups as a whole approximate closely the aggregate of the more detailed groups. Since almost none of this employment works shifts, *all of its employment* is listed under no-shift industries.[7]

The third line under each year refers to what I have called somewhat loosely continuous industries. These industries are represented by the following:

Industry	Standard Industrial Classification Code
Pulp, paper, and paperboard mills	261, 262, and 263
Industrial chemicals including synthetic fibers	28, except 283, 284, 285, and 289
Petroleum and petroleum products	29
Basic iron and steel	331
Primary nonferrous metals	333

The steel and chemicals groups are somewhat broader than desired, and the list above does not contain a few smaller continuously operating industries such as beet sugar. Using the broader groups, however, facilitated the task of obtaining time series on employment.[8]

For each of these continuous industries there was a recent BLS Industry Wage Survey showing the proportion of workers in late shifts, except for the primary nonferrous metal industry, for which a World War II study had to be used. For a given industry I decided to use a fixed proportion for the share of its production worker employment on late shifts because I was not certain that the small variations in the share from one survey to another had any statistical significance and, besides, I did not have an exact matching of years between a given industry's employment, on the one hand, and the appropriate Industry Wage Survey, on the other. If the proportions of total employment on late shifts for the continuous group had increased over time, the use of fixed proportions would bias upward the trend in the proportion applicable to the noncontinuous group. In fact there seems to be no pattern in the behavior of the proportions over time. For example, using the closest estimate of 1952 late-shift proportions in place of what I actually used for 1952 gave virtually the same results.

The employment on late shifts for all-other manufacturing (line 4 under each year)—that is, manufacturing excluding the no-shift and the continuous groups—is obtained as a residual. For that line the proportions shown in column 2 are equal to column 3 divided by column 1. From 1952 to 1978–1979 the proportion of late-shift workers in this group rose much more than the late-shift proportion in all manufacturing: from 22.96 percent to 31.03 percent, or by 35.1 percent, as against a comparable figure of 28.7 percent for all manufacturing. In fact, from 1952 to 1978–1979, total production worker employment in the all-other group more than accounted for the rise in production worker employment in manufacturing (see table 14). Furthermore, about four-fifths of the employment rise in all-other manufacturing reflected employment of workers on late shifts. These developments show up with even greater force in the later period than in the earlier period.

Unfortunately the data pertaining to metropolitan areas could not be extended back beyond 1951 or 1952. Consequently it was necessary to resort to data from Industry Wage Surveys. The BLS conducted a number of industry surveys in manufacturing late during World War II and early in the postwar period. These surveys were presented in

TABLE 14

INCREASES IN PRODUCTION WORKER EMPLOYMENT, BY SHIFT STATUS OF INDUSTRY, 1952 TO 1978–1979 (millions)

	1952–1969	1969–1978/79	1952–1978/79
Total manufacturing industries	1.41	0.13	1.54
Industries using noncontinuous shifts[a]	1.30	0.37	1.67
Workers on late shifts	0.93	0.42	1.35
Workers on day shifts	0.37	−0.05	0.32

a. "All-other" in table 13.
SOURCE: Author, based on BLS statistics.

summary form in BLS Bulletin 939, *Supplementary Wage Practices in American Industry, 1945-46*. I did not think it advisable to compare the summary figure from this compilation (24 percent) for the 1945–1946 period with the metropolitan area average for 1952 because there were problems of comparability in industry coverage. I did, however, make use of the results for a large subcategory designated "metalworking" and for particular industries outside metalworking.

For metalworking I concluded, after examining some independent BLS data on shift work collected in another survey made during the Korean War,[9] that there was no change in the proportion of workers on late shifts from 1945–1946 to 1952. I also made some comparisons for food, cigarettes, textiles, lumber, paper products (other than pulp, paper, and board), and chemicals. These yielded a small rise in the proportion of workers on late shifts from 1945–1946 to 1952. All told the sample industries yielded a rise of 2 percent (not percentage points) in the late-shift proportion. This figure was used to represent the change in the late-shift employment proportion for all-other manufacturing. The 1945–1946 figure and the proportions for the four points discussed earlier are given in the first column of table 15.

Translating Shift Proportions into Plant Hours. The next task was to translate figures pertaining to the proportion of production workers on late shifts into average weekly plant hours. This was accomplished through the use of a simple "bridge" equation:

$$y = a + bx \qquad (1)$$

TABLE 15

PROPORTIONS OF PRODUCTION WORKERS EMPLOYED ON LATE SHIFTS AND ESTIMATED AVERAGE WEEKLY PLANT HOURS, ALL-OTHER MANUFACTURING INDUSTRIES, 1945 TO 1978–1979

	On Late Shifts (%)	Estimated Average Weekly Plant Hours
1945/46	22.5	76.7
1952	23.0	77.3
1959/60	23.8	78.5
1969	28.4	84.6
1978/79	31.0	88.2

SOURCE: Column 1: table 13 and text. Column 2: text.

where y is average weekly plant hours and x is the proportion of all plant workers employed on late shifts. The data for the y values were the basic census data pertaining to the fourth quarter of 1976 used in the first study.[10] The data for the x values came from individual industry wage surveys published by the BLS. By covering a broad range of industries, one should be able to observe how weekly plant hours increase as the proportion of workers on late shifts increases. I left out continuous industries, however, because industries that work essentially around the clock have differing proportions of workers on late shifts, depending on disparate factors such as maintenance, transportation, and so forth. Altogether I had thirty-one observations with a median survey date in the fall of 1975.[11]

These observations yielded the equation

$$y = 46.4 + 1.347x$$
$$(10.3) \quad (8.3)$$

with t-statistics shown in parentheses. The coefficient of determination corrected for degrees of freedom is .695.

The constant is the equivalent of average weekly plant hours of plants in which no shift work is ordinarily employed. The average is more than forty hours because there may be some overtime or a little maintenance work performed after normal hours. It agrees fairly closely with combined average weekly plant hours for apparel, leather, and furniture for the fourth quarter of 1976.

Applying the coefficients in the equation to the proportions shown in the first column of table 15 yields the estimated average weekly plant hours for all-other manufacturing shown in the second column.

These estimates of average weekly plant hours applicable to all-other manufacturing have to be related to the 24.7 percent rise in average weekly plant hours for all manufacturing from 1929 to 1976 (see table 8). This connection is shown in the bottom part of table 16, which is broken down in greater detail in table 17. Some alternative estimates, however, are presented in the top part of table 16, which reflects the construction of averages with varying capital weights and is identical with line B of table 8. To derive all-other manufacturing we subtract from the manufacturing total the one-shift and the continuous industries in those years, first with 1929 weights and then with 1976 weights. This method yields an estimate of average weekly plant hours of 90.2 hours in 1976, which may be compared with an estimate of 87.0 hours derived through the use of proportions of workers on late shifts and equation 1.

The bottom part of table 16, based on the overall change of 24.7 percent, reflects the use of fixed 1954 weights based on real gross fixed

TABLE 16

AVERAGE WEEKLY PLANT HOURS AND THEIR CHANGE IN
MANUFACTURING INDUSTRIES, BY SHIFT STATUS OF INDUSTRY,
1929–1976

Shift Status of Industry	1929	1976	Change (hours)	Change (%)
Changing Weights[a]				
Total manufacturing	91.90	110.3	18.4	20.0[b]
Continuous	136.40	157.8	21.4	15.7
No-shift	49.20	48.9	−0.3	−0.6
All-other	66.92	90.2	23.3	34.8
Fixed Weights[c]				
Total manufacturing				24.7[d]
Continuous				10.8
No-shift				0
All-other				32.4

a. Horsepower in 1929; gross fixed assets in 1976. See tables 8 and 9.
b. Same as table 8, variant B.
c. Fixed weights (real gross fixed assets in 1954) applied to 1929–1976 change for each industry.
d. Same as table 8, variant C.
SOURCE: Author.

assets. Note that the no-shift industries show no change on average over this period. I would hazard a guess that average weekly plant hours of these industries as a group experienced a dip from 1929 to, say, the late 1940s and then rose slightly as a few companies adopted shift work. The continuous industries show a rise of 10.8 percent (see table 17). For some, like petroleum, there is scarcely any change, but others experienced increases. The paper industry was on a six-day week until the 1940s, when the industry shifted to a seven-day week over the next decade or so.[12] The continuous part of chemicals increased in importance from 1929 to 1976. The integrated steel industry employs continuous processes in the production of coke (coke ovens), iron (blast furnaces), and steel ingots (melting furnaces); but the rolling and finishing of steel have not necessarily been around-the-clock operations throughout the week. I interpret the rise in average hours to be a reflection of technological developments—the continuous hot strip mill (introduced around 1941) and continuous cold rolling—but I have not examined this occurrence in detail.[13]

TABLE 17

Derivation of Percentage Change in Average Weekly Plant Hours for All-Other Manufacturing Industries, 1929–1976

	1954 Weight[a] (millions)	Change (%)
Total manufacturing	172,491	24.7
Less continuous industries[b]	54,943	10.8
Paper	6,041	17.8
Chemicals	7,980	16.5
Petroleum	16,090	1.1
Stone	1,650	7.8
Primary metals	23,182	14.0
Less no-shift industries	4,194	0.0
Apparel	1,694	0.6
Leather	1,036	−7.7
Furniture	1,464	4.6
Equals all-other manufacturing	113,354	32.4

NOTE: This table breaks down into greater detail the data in the bottom of table 16.
a. Gross fixed assets in 1972 dollars as estimated by BLS.
b. Continuous portions as reflected in detailed industry average weekly plant hours.
SOURCES: Percentage changes: author, based on census data. Weights from BLS.

The residual method just described yields an increase of 32.4 percent from 1929 to 1976 in average weekly plant hours for all-other manufacturing. The next problem is to interpolate between the two years.

1. For the all-other-manufacturing group, selected points from 1945–1946 to 1978–1979 are shown in table 15. The estimate for 1976 was obtained by interpolation. Subtracting the change from 1945–1946 to 1976 from the forty-seven-year change from 1929 to 1976 leaves a residual for the period 1929 to 1945–1946. Straight-line interpolation was used to obtain years between 1929 and 1945–1946.

2. One-shift industries were assumed to be unchanged over the entire period.

3. For continuous industries a few bits of information made possible some rough judgments concerning changes in average weekly plant hours. The paper industry was estimated to change from a six-day to a seven-day week in a straight line from 1945 to 1955. Thereafter no change was assumed. Steel plant hours were assumed to in-

TABLE 18

Changes and Annual Rates of Change in Average Weekly Plant Hours in Manufacturing, 1929–1976

Period	Total Manufacturing		All-Other Manufacturing	
	% change	Annual rate of change (%)	% change	Annual rate of change (%)
1929–1976	24.7[a]	0.47	32.4[a]	0.60
1929–1945/46	11.4	0.66	16.4	0.92
1945/46–1976	11.9	0.37	13.7	0.42
1945/46–1952	1.4	0.21	0.8	0.12
1952–1959/60	1.6	0.22	1.5	0.20
1959/60–1969	5.9	0.60	7.8	0.79
1969–1978/79	3.4	0.36	4.2	0.44
1969–1976	2.5	0.37	3.1	0.44

a. See table 17.
Source: Author.

46

crease steadily because of continuousness in rolling and finishing starting in 1940. For chemicals, petroleum, and stone a linear trend throughout was assumed. Again using 1954 weights, I combined the three groups to obtain the indexes of average weekly plant hours for manufacturing shown in table 1.

Results

If the forty-seven years are divided into two periods—1929 to 1945–1946 and 1945–1946 to 1976—the overall changes in average weekly plant hours are about the same, but the compounded annual rate of change is considerably greater for the prewar period than for the postwar period (see table 18). From the end of the war to about 1960, growth in average weekly plant hours was quite small. During the 1960s growth speeded up considerably, but from 1969 to 1978–1979 it slowed down. The annual rate of change from 1969 to 1978–1979 was about average for the postwar period.

There is a suggestion from table 10 that some of the national retardation of the 1970s evident in that table is a reflection of developments on the West Coast. The change may reflect a long-run regional change possibly associated with defense and space production or with the aircraft industry. But this gets into an explanation of the differences in rates of change over time, which is discussed in the next chapter.

Notes

1. See Murray F. Foss, *Changes in the Workweek of Fixed Capital: U.S. Manufacturing, 1929 to 1976* (Washington, D.C.: American Enterprise Institute, 1981), pp. 1–20.

2. Various adjustments are discussed in ibid., pp. 17–21.

3. For a substantial but partial listing, see U.S. Department of Labor, Bureau of Labor Statistics, *Directory of Occupational Wage Surveys, Jan. 1950–Dec. 1975*, Report 468 (1976), pp. 8–26.

4. See ibid., pp. 31–121, for studies in the 1950–1975 period.

5. For a recent summary see U.S. Department of Labor, BLS, *Area Wage Surveys, Metropolitan Areas, United States and Regional Summaries, 1977* (October 1980), p. 103. The rising trend evident in these figures from about 1960 to the 1970s has been noted by other investigators. See, for example, S. J. Prais, *Productivity and Industrial Structure* (Cambridge: Cambridge University Press, 1981), p. 301. See earlier references in note 1, chap. 3.

6. These data were used by Taubman and Gottschalk to construct a quarterly series on plant utilization from 1952 through 1968. See Paul Taubman and Peter Gottschalk, "The Average Workweek of Capital in Manufacturing,"

Journal of the American Statistical Association, vol. 66, no. 335 (September 1971), pp. 448–55.

7. This is a simplification. The leather-tanning industry works shifts, as does the work clothing industry, but these were judged small enough to ignore.

8. It is possible that the omission of smaller continuous industries, especially new industries, has biased the results shown here, but I have no evidence that it has done so.

9. BLS, "Employment and Shift Operations in Metalworking Industries" (Unpublished preliminary paper, April 1951).

10. See Foss, *Changes in the Workweek of Fixed Capital*, pp. 7–10.

11. See Appendix H for list of industries and data. The limiting factor in this comparison was the availability of Industry Wage Surveys either embracing or within a few years of the fourth quarter of 1976.

12. Letter from Mr. David L. Luke III, President, Westvaco Corp., October 1980.

13. If the continuous group were to show zero change from 1929 to 1976, the overall change for manufacturing would drop to 20 percent, but that is clearly an extreme assumption.

3

Evaluating the Manufacturing Results for Interim Years

Other Manufacturing Data

Lack of data makes independent checks of the results in chapter 2 difficult. For the post–World War II period some data are available from the Industry Wage Surveys conducted by the Bureau of Labor Statistics. Unfortunately the industry coverage is somewhat limited, and constructing time series from the surveys is not easy. In 1970 Charles O'Connor of the BLS called attention to the increasing proportions of workers on late shifts as revealed in the Industry Wage Surveys.[1] Using all the data available through 1980, I was able to compare for twenty-six individual industries the proportion of all production workers employed on late shifts in an early postwar year with the corresponding proportion in the 1970s. Excluding continuous industries, the early period (approximately 1946) yielded an unweighted average of 19.9 percent, whereas the later period (approximately 1974) yielded an average of 27.5 percent. The average annual rate of change compounded over the twenty-eight years was 1.16 percent. This annual rate may be compared to an annual change of 0.97 percent on the basis of the metropolitan area data described in chapter 2 (table 15). These particular figures are unweighted and refer to proportions of production workers on late shifts (see table 19).

How do the chapter 2 estimates for 1945–1946 compare with independent estimates for the same period and with the two benchmark years? A study by the BLS pertaining to 1945 and 1946 showed that 24 percent of production workers in manufacturing were employed on late shifts.[2] Although the study was based on a large number of reports for individual industries, the results would not necessarily be the same as those based on a probability sample. The 24 percent is somewhat higher than the extrapolated figure of 22.5 percent obtained from the metropolitan area data discussed above; however, it is clearly below the peak postwar figure of the late 1970s. Considering that the 1945–1946 average reflected to some extent an intensive use of

TABLE 19

PROPORTION OF MANUFACTURING PRODUCTION WORKERS EMPLOYED ON LATE SHIFTS, POST–WORLD WAR II:
COMPARISON OF RESULTS FROM TWO SOURCES, 1945–1946 TO 1978–1979

	Early		*Later*		*Increase* (%)	*Annual Rate of Change* (%)
	Year	%	Year	%		
26 Industry Wage Surveys	1946	19.9	1974	27.5	38.3	1.16
Metropolitan areas (all-other manufacturing)	1945–46	22.5	1978–79	31.0	37.8	0.97

SOURCE: See text, especially table 15.

fixed capital that firms might not have undertaken except for the urgency of wartime conditions, these particular figures for the late war–early postwar period do not appear to be unreasonable when reviewed in relation to 1976.

We can also roughly compare the 1945–1946 results with those of 1929. The Bureau of the Census has made special tabulations of the 1929 Census of Manufactures data according to whether plants were one-shift, two-shift, or three or more shifts.[3] Excluding the one-shift and continuous industries from the all-manufacturing total yields the following:

	Wage-Earner Employment (millions)		
Total	1-shift plants	2-shift plants	3-shift plants
6.4	5.2	0.9	0.3

Now suppose one makes an extreme assumption, namely, that employment in two-shift plants is equally divided between the first and second shifts and employment in three-shift plants is equally divided among the first, second, and third shifts. This assumption is extreme because all the evidence suggests that the first shift has a disproportionately large share of employment.[4] Even with this assumption, it appears that less than 10 percent of employment in industries exclusive of continuous and one-shift industries worked late shifts in 1929 $[(0.5 + 0.1) \div 6.4]$.

	Type of Plant (%)			
Employment on	1-shift	2-shift	3-shift	*Total*
1st shift	5.2	0.45	0.10	5.8
2d shift	0	0.45	0.10	0.5
3d shift	0	0	0.10	0.1
				6.4

One hesitates to conclude much more than that the proportion of workers on late shifts showed a very large increase from 1929 to the mid-1940s, which seems to have been much larger than the change from the mid-1940s to the late 1970s.

National Industrial Conference Board Surveys. The National Industrial Conference Board (NICB) canvassed a group of 130 large companies in 1937 to obtain information on shift patterns.[5] For our purposes a few facts are important. The firms employed 229,000 persons in October 1937, of whom 61,000 were in continuous and 167,000 were in noncontinuous industries; of the latter, machines and machine tools, textiles and clothing, other metal products, and electrical appliances accounted for 90 percent. Of the noncontinuous group, sixty-seven companies had adopted shift work as a permanent policy, seven had adopted it as permanent in some departments but not in others, and thirty had adopted it temporarily. Work on late shifts was reported for 17 percent of the companies in noncontinuous operations. The figure for late-shift work would undoubtedly be much lower for firms of all sizes, roughly between the "less than 10 percent" mentioned on the preceding page and the 22.5 percent obtained for 1945–1946 as shown in table 15. Unfortunately we do not know how the 130 companies were chosen for the sample.

Results of a survey conducted by the same organization in 1927 are given in table 20 for manufacturing firms.[6] This survey also shows that less than 10 percent of employment in noncontinuous industries was in night work. That figure ties in with the estimates derived above from the 1929 census, but, as with the 1937 survey, information regarding the sample is scarce.[7] Average firm size is quite large for the sample (over 3,000 employees per firm); and, given the direct relation between size and use of shift work, the results from the NICB sample undoubtedly yield too high a figure for manufacturing as a whole.

Textiles. The textile industry is perhaps unique in providing statistics on the use of capital by shift as well as on capital hours.[8] Aside from year-to-year changes caused by shifts in demand and the bulge brought on by World War II, the trend was strongly upward until the mid-1960s, after which hours either leveled off or declined a little. Data for selected periods appear in the table below, which omits years that were unduly depressed because of demand.

	Average Annual Hours per Spindle
1926–1929	3,147
1936–1937 and 1939–1940	4,105
1945–1946[9]	5,072
1972–1974 and 1976	6,304

Table 21 shows five-year averages of spindle hours from the mid-1920s and similar data for cotton looms starting in the mid-1940s. To judge from the figures in the last two columns, the industry operated virtually two full shifts in 1944 and reached a three-shift basis by the late 1950s. In fact, the spindle hours suggest that two-shift operations were reached by the late 1930s, since an eighty-hour week (two shifts of eight hours each, five days a week) for fifty weeks would yield four thousand hours per year, which was almost attained in 1936–1937.[10]

TABLE 20
NIGHT WORKERS AS PERCENTAGE OF TOTAL EMPLOYMENT, SAMPLE STUDY, 1927

	Total Employees (thousands)	Night Workers (thousands)	Night Workers (%)
Rotating shifts (continuous industries)	202.3	35.4	17.5
Fixed shifts (noncontinuous industries)	397.7	35.5	8.9
Regular policy	318.0	28.8	9.0
Temporary policy	79.7	6.7	8.4
Total	600.0	70.9	11.8

SOURCE: National Industrial Conference Board, *Night Work in Industry* (New York: NICB, 1927).

TABLE 21

COTTON SYSTEM: AVERAGE ANNUAL HOURS OF OPERATION PER
SPINDLE AND PER LOOM AND PERCENTAGE OF LOOMS ON SECOND AND
THIRD SHIFTS, 1925–1979

	Annual Hours		% of 1st-Shift Cotton Looms[a] on	
	Per spindle[b]	Per loom[c]	Second shift	Third shift
1925–29	3,097			
1930–34	3,070			
1935–39	3,748			
1940–44	5,231		92.3	26.8
1945–49	5,163	5,183[d]	98.3	68.8
1950–54	5,728	5,922	99.5	87.6
1955–59	6,046	6,162	99.8	97.0
1960–64	6,361	6,337	99.7	99.3
1965–69	6,533	6,671	99.6	99.0
1970–74	6,238	6,546	99.7	98.3
1975–79	6,103	6,390		

NOTE: Spindles and looms account for a large part of the equipment in an integrated cotton mill. According to the Census Bureau, in 1976 cotton looms worked an average of 125 hours per week and cotton spindles 119.5 hours per week. These figures are a little lower than the completely independent figure of 126.1 hours per week that the cotton textile industry operated according to the basic census survey used for the derivation of average weekly plant hours.
a. Data refer to last year in the interval.
b. Data before August 1945 relate to spindles consuming 100 percent cotton only. The switch to "all fibers" after August 1945 does not have a material effect on the comparability of the series.
c. Weekly average for month times 52.
d. 1946–1949.
SOURCES: Column 1: U.S. Department of Commerce, Bureau of the Census, as reported in various issues of *Survey of Current Business*. Annual hours per spindle reflect spindle hours divided by number of active spindles. Columns 2, 3, and 4: *Textile HI-LIGHTS*, various quarterly issues, American Textile Manufacturers Institute.

Statistical Issues

This study (see chapter 2) used standard metropolitan statistical area (SMSA) data from the BLS showing the proportion of workers on late shifts as indirect interpolators of average weekly plant hours from 1976 back to 1952. The question we face is whether these SMSA figures are biased.

SMSAs have not been constant in makeup. In its area wage surveys BLS accepts boundaries of SMSAs as defined by the Office of Management and Budget for a certain number of years, after which it switches to a more up-to-date definition. There has been an increasing tendency for SMSAs to embrace outlying counties. Conceivably the observed upward trend over time in the proportion of workers on late shifts within a given metropolitan area is a reflection of conditions in areas newly added to the SMSA. Insofar as the "new" area contains plants that did not exist before, there is no problem. But if the upward trend means simply that the BLS in a sense (because of the new boundaries) is belatedly picking up late-shift plants that might have been embraced earlier with a constant area definition of an SMSA, then the rise over time in the proportion of workers on late shifts is illusory. But I do not know a good way of checking this.

A more serious potential problem concerns the trend of manufacturing employment in the SMSAs. The Bureau of Economic Analysis has prepared estimates of employment based on constant definitions of SMSAs. That is, since the boundaries of SMSAs have been constantly expanding, the BEA takes today's (expanded) definition of SMSAs and traces back over time the employment of identical counties. Table 22 compares employment in SMSA and non-SMSA counties for all private wage and salary workers, on the one hand, and for manufacturing, on the other. From 1967 to 1978 private wage and salary employment in SMSA counties grew 26 percent and in non-SMSA counties grew 36 percent. But for manufacturing the SMSA group was virtually at the same level in 1978 as in 1967, whereas the non-SMSA counties rose by 22 percent. Conceivably the failure of the SMSA counties to show any growth in manufacturing employment from 1967 to 1978 could be a reflection of different industry mixes. Possibly the SMSA counties experienced a growth in capital-intensive industries whereas the non-SMSA counties experienced growth in labor-intensive industries. But that conclusion would be rather far-fetched since the SMSA counties in 1967 accounted for almost 80 percent of total manufacturing employment. More likely, the SMSAs are enjoying less economic growth and less investment than the rest of the country. A check of seventy-nine large SMSAs (those with at least 40,000 manufacturing employees) showed that they accounted for 54.6 percent of production worker employment but for only 51.4 percent of capital expenditures, according to figures from the 1972 Census of Manufactures. An implication of these figures is that the BLS metropolitan data are not capturing the most modern plants employing "best" manufacturing practice and may be missing plants where shift work is most prevalent.[11] And it is possible that the use of SMSA data has understated the growth of shift work in noncontinu-

TABLE 22

EMPLOYMENT IN SMSA AND NON-SMSA COUNTIES, IN PRIVATE NONFARM AND MANUFACTURING INDUSTRIES, 1967–1978

	Private Nonfarm Wage and Salary Workers[a] (millions)		Index of Manufacturing Employment	
	SMSA counties	Non-SMSA counties	SMSA counties	Non-SMSA counties
1967	46.5	11.1	100	100
1968	47.8	11.4	102	103
1969	49.3	11.8	103	107
1970	49.0	11.8	98	105
1971	48.7	12.0	93	104
1972	50.1	12.5	95	109
1973	52.5	13.2	99	117
1974	53.1	13.4	99	117
1975	51.5	13.1	91	106
1976	53.1	13.8	94	113
1977	55.4	14.4	97	118
1978	58.5	15.2	101	122

NOTE: SMSA = standard metropolitan statistical area.
a. Data include full-time and part-time workers.
SOURCE: Bureau of Economic Analysis.

ous industries over the postwar years and, as a consequence, that I have given too much importance to such growth in the years from 1929 to 1945–1946.

Economic Issues

This study shows that the rise in average weekly plant hours in manufacturing was somewhat greater—and much greater in terms of *annual* rates of change—from 1929 to the early post–World War II period than from that period to 1976. Looking at these findings in broad terms, one can ask, What are the economic factors supporting or opposing these conclusions?

Capital Stock. In arguing against this position, one could adduce the very low rate of fixed investment during the 1930s and in the civilian goods industries during the war. As estimated by the BEA, real gross stocks of structures and equipment in manufacturing were only 21 percent higher in 1948 than in 1929. In contrast, labor input was 37 percent higher and output 84 percent greater, according to John Kendrick.[12] This small growth in the capital stock could be important because the decision by businessmen to use shifts is ordinarily part of the investment decision and, if the BEA's stock estimates are correct, at the end of the war not only did business have a small stock of fixed capital, but only a part of that stock may have been well adapted to the use of multiple shifts under the market conditions of a peacetime economy. To the extent that this line of argument is correct, it might imply that the estimated rise in plant hours from 1929 to the early postwar years is overstated and that more of the rise should be allocated to the postwar period. Other factors favoring shift work, however, were operating.

Regional Trends. Although the 1930s were depression years, they were also years of considerable movement and innovation as firms sought to cope with the vast shrinkage in demand. A notable feature of the 1930s was the shift in fixed capital to the South (table 23). In 1929 the South accounted for 18.8 percent of manufacturing horsepower, but in 1939 this proportion had risen to 27.0 percent; on balance the South accounted for almost two-thirds of the net increase in U.S manufacturing horsepower over the decade. Interestingly, the South's share of horsepower in place remained unchanged from 1939 to 1954 and did not resume its increase until the mid-1950s.

The move of capital to the South signifies more than just a move from relatively high-wage areas to low-wage areas. In all likelihood

TABLE 23

MANUFACTURING HORSEPOWER IN THE SOUTH, 1929–1962
(percentage of U.S. manufacturing horsepower)

Year	Percent
1929	18.8
1939	27.0
1954	26.9
1962	29.6

NOTE: South includes East South Central, West South Central, and South Atlantic states.
SOURCE: Census of Manufactures.

the move was made also because capital could be used more intensively in the South than in the three other regions of the country. In 1929, for example, the South led the three other regions in the proportions of employment in plants operating two or more shifts (see table 24).[13]

Size of Plant. Although shift work was not common in 1929, it was most prevalent among the largest plants and least prevalent among the smallest plants (see table 25). Rising plant size within industries would be accompanied by greater prevalence of shift work.

A corollary of the rise in plant size was the decline in the importance of single-plant firms. The hypothesis is that in a small manufac-

TABLE 24

DISTRIBUTION OF EMPLOYMENT IN MANUFACTURING, 1929
(percent)

Region	Fewer Than 2 Shifts	2 or More Shifts
Northeast	82	18
North Central	79	21
South	71	29
West	75	25

SOURCE: Foss, *Changes in the Workweek of Fixed Capital*, p. 31.

TABLE 25

AVERAGE PLANT OPERATIONS, BY VALUE-ADDED CLASS, 1929 AND 1976

	Less Than $100,000	$100,000– 999,999	$1,000,000– 4,999,999	$5,000,000 and Over
1929				
Number of shifts	1.2	1.2	1.4	1.5
Hours per day	10.3	11.0	12.5	12.9
Days per week	5.7	5.7	5.8	5.9
Hours per week	58.9	62.7	72.9	75.7
1976				
Number of shifts	1.1	1.2	1.7	2.2
Hours per day	9.2	10.2	13.6	18.2
Days per week	5.1	5.1	5.2	5.5
Hours per week	47.1	51.5	69.8	100.0

SOURCE: U.S. Department of Commerce, Bureau of the Census, unpublished data.

turing business the owner considers his presence to be important for the profitable functioning of the business or thinks that the cost of hiring a manager to supervise a late shift is uneconomic. If this hypothesis is valid, shift work will either be absent or be severely limited in small firms.[14] As this type of organization decreases in importance, this constraint on the use of shift work is diminished. In my earlier study support for this hypothesis was found in cross-sectional regression analysis for both 1929 and 1976 as well as in the analyses of the change from 1929 to 1976.[15] Support—at a point of time and over time—also comes from some BLS studies of the meat industry for 1963 and 1979 (see table 26). Not only are late-shift proportions higher in multiplant firms than in single-plant firms in each year, but the patterns over time are quite different. Over the sixteen years from 1963 to 1979 the single-plant meatpacking firms show relatively little or no change in the proportions of workers on late shifts, whereas the multiplant firms show large increases in the proportions. A similar but not quite so striking pattern is evident in the prepared-meat industry.

Table 27 shows the proportion of value added in manufacturing accounted for by single-unit firms. The data are interesting for a number of reasons. They show a pronounced decline in the single-unit share of value added from 1929 to 1939, the rate of decline exceeding the average rate of decrease from 1939 to 1977. There was a reversal of

TABLE 26

PERCENTAGE OF PRODUCTION WORKERS IN MEAT INDUSTRIES ON LATE
SHIFTS, 1963 AND 1979

Type of Firm	1963	1979
Meatpacking: total	10.7	17.1
Multiplant	13.6	22.4
Single-plant	6.5	6.8
Prepared meats: total	11.7	18.5
Multiplant	17.4	27.1
Single-plant	8.4	10.4

SOURCE: BLS Bulletin 1415 (November 1963) and BLS Bulletin 2082 (December 1980).

the long-term trend between 1939 and 1947, probably because of the huge numbers of small businesses established by war veterans aided by the GI bill. But by 1954 the downward trend was resumed and has shown up in each succeeding Census of Manufactures. It is interesting that this decline in manufacturing stands in contrast to the relative stability of the single-unit ratio in retail trade from 1929 to 1954, as table 28 indicates.

Effects of the Wage-Hour Law and the War. My earlier study found that those industries most vulnerable to the premium-pay-for-overtime provisions of the Wage-Hour Law enacted at the end of 1938 were the most likely to adopt shift work.[16] "Vulnerable" industries were those with long average weekly hours for labor *before* the new law. For a given level of output the changeover to shift work had to be prompt if the penalty overtime rates were to be avoided. By itself the changeover would not immediately alter average weekly plant hours. Faced with the necessity of expanding output in the long run, however, firms either had to expand the use of shift work in existing facilities or had to build new plants. Firms had the option of building larger plants designed for one-shift operation or smaller plants designed for multiple shifts. In other words, firms that had some experience with multiple-shift operations continued along that route in building new plants or in expanding shift work in existing plants. Firms lacking the experience chose the larger plant–one shift route.

Several factors eased the transition. First, the potential drop in output occasioned by the reduction in the length of the workweek may not have been of immediate concern because demand and output

TABLE 27

SHARE OF MANUFACTURING VALUE ADDED ACCOUNTED FOR BY SINGLE-UNIT FIRMS, 1929–1977

	Value Added ($ billion)		Single-Unit Share of Total (%)	Annual Rate of Change in Single-Unit Share from Preceding Period
	Single-unit firms	Total manufacturing		
1929[a]	15.8	30.6	51.8	—
1939	9.8	24.7	39.7	-2.6
1947	30.3	74.3	40.8	0.3
1954	37.4	117.0	32.0	-3.4
1958	37.8	143.2	26.4	-4.7
1963	45.5	192.1	23.7	-2.1
1967	52.5[b]	262.0	20.0	-4.2
1972	67.9	354.0	19.2	-0.8
1977	100.1	585.2	17.1	-2.3
1929–1977				-2.3
1939–1977				-2.2

NOTE: In 1947 and earlier years, "single-unit" meant that the firm consisted of a single manufacturing plant but that it might operate other establishments in nonmanufacturing industries. After 1947 "single-unit" meant that the firm consisted solely of the single establishment in manufacturing.

a. Excludes railroad repair shops and manufactured gas.

b. Excludes small firms tabulated through administrative records. Inclusion of such firms would raise total to $55.5 billion, or 21.2 percent.

SOURCE: Basic data from Census of Manufactures.

TABLE 28

RELATIVE IMPORTANCE OF SINGLE-UNIT FIRMS IN MANUFACTURING AND
IN RETAIL TRADE, 1929–1954

(percent)

	Manufacturing[a]	Retail Trade[b]
1929	51.8	68.6
1939	39.7	65.2
1947	40.8	70.3
1954	32.0	69.9

a. Percentage of value added accounted for by single-unit firms.
b. Percentage of retail sales accounted for by single-unit firms.
SOURCE: Calculations by author based on data from Census of Manufactures and Census of Business.

were so depressed in the 1930s (although output began to rise in 1933). Second, the National Recovery Act (NRA), which was effective from 1933 to 1935, helped for several industries. That is, the adjustment to a lower level of weekly labor hours really began with the NRA legislation rather than in 1938. Third, firms gained experience in operating multiple shifts during World War II because of wartime pressures.

Wage Differentials for Late Shifts. Firms resort to shift work because they want to economize in their use of capital. To attract labor to work evenings and nights, however, they may be forced to pay a wage differential, which will act as a restraint on the use of late shifts. Wage differentials for shift work in the United States are not large, currently averaging about 4–5 percent of straight-time wages in manufacturing.[17] Moreover, figures available from the BLS since about 1959 have pointed to a decline on shift differentials in relation to straight-time hourly wages.[18] Indeed, some very limited information—from the printing trades, where night work on newspapers has traditionally commanded premiums over day work—suggests that since 1929 at least the relative trend of the night differential has been downward.[19] A decline in the shift differential should act to encourage shift work. The paragraphs that follow provide information on shift differentials for the period covered by this study.

The trend of wage differentials in relation to straight-time earnings from 1959–1960 to 1980, based on annual BLS wage surveys of metropolitan areas, is illustrated in figure 2. The movement is unmistakably downward for both second- and third-shift differentials.

For the period between the end of World War II and 1959–1960 only a single study, applicable to the years 1945–1946, is available at the moment. It suggests that the differential *rose* from the end of the war to 1959–1960. This rise reflected two influences. Although the differential itself rose less than straight-time wages, the proportion of firms (weighted by employment) working shifts and paying a differential increased substantially—from perhaps 57 percent to approximately 95 percent.[20] A comparison of the two is given in table 29.

Other available data pertain to *provisions* in union contracts. Provisions for payment are not the same as differentials actually paid, but

FIGURE 2

LATE-SHIFT WAGE DIFFERENTIALS IN MANUFACTURING, 1961–1980

(percentage of straight-time average hourly earnings)

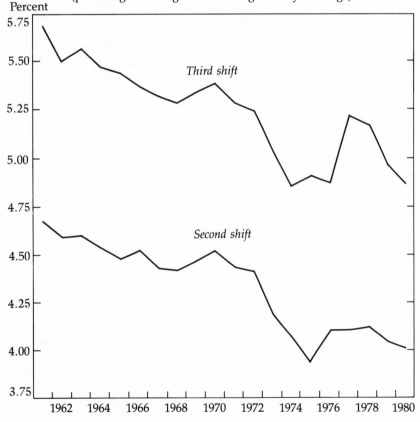

SOURCE: Basic data from Bureau of Labor Statistics.

TABLE 29
LATE-SHIFT WAGE DIFFERENTIALS IN MANUFACTURING, 1945–1946 AND 1959–1960
(percentage of straight-time hourly wage)

	Second Shift			Third Shift		
	Differential of firms paying	Percent paying	Differential of all firms working shifts	Differential of firms paying	Percent paying	Differential of all firms working shifts
1945–1946	6.4	57	3.6	7.4	63	4.7
1959–1960	5.1	94	4.8	6.0	95	5.7

NOTE: The industries covered account for about one-half of manufacturing employment and omit basic steel, petroleum, printing, lumber, rubber, and shipbuilding.

SOURCES: Calculations by author on the basis of BLS data. Bureau of Labor Statistics, *Supplementary Wage Practices in American Industry, 1945/46*, Bulletin 939. Also O'Connor, "Late Shift Employment in Manufacturing Industries," p. 37. Wage differentials cited by O'Connor reflect those paid in metropolitan areas.

obviously the two are related. An examination of union contracts by the BLS showed a rising trend in the *provision* for shift differentials in manufacturing. In 1943, for example, 70 percent of workers under union agreements regarding shift work were provided late-shift wage differentials. By 1952 this proportion had risen to 96 percent and by 1958 to 97 percent.[21] This trend was given considerable impetus in late 1944–early 1945 by a decision of the National War Labor Board (WLB).[22] The board had initially maintained that differentials for shift work in continuous industries like basic iron and steel were unnecessary because the steel industry employed rotating shifts,[23] and the board felt that any premium pay for night work in essence might be reflected in the basic wage. Although this practice used to be common, the specific case at hand was one in which the board found no difference in wages between workers on fixed shifts and workers on rotating shifts. The problem arose from competitive forces outside the industry. Under pressure to expand production during the war, many noncontinuous industries adopted shift work and paid premiums in order to attract labor on late shifts. Continuous industries, which had to compete in the labor market with noncontinuous industries, thus found it necessary to pay premiums also. Because the steel industry had no experience in paying shift differentials, the WLB set a differential of $0.04 for the second shift and $0.06 for the third shift. For noncontinuous industries the differentials approved were $0.04 and $0.08. At that time (April 1945) straight-time wages were $0.956 per hour.

Two other studies that are of some help come from surveys applicable to 1927 and October 1937 conducted by the National Industrial Conference Board (NICB).[24] These studies show a decline in the differential over this ten-year period, which is hardly surprising given the existence of high unemployment in 1937 despite the recovery in economic activity after 1932. The experience of 1927–1937 appears to be somewhat different from that of the postwar period since in the early period we find a sharp decline in the differential paid by those firms paying a differential and only a small decline in the proportion of firms (weighted by employment) paying the differential (see first two lines of table 30).

The results shown in table 30 tie in with answers to other parts of the NICB questionnaires. When respondents were asked about difficulties in recruiting workers for night work, 42 percent of the respondents in the 1927 survey indicated that they experienced difficulties, but only 11 percent of the respondents in the 1937 survey answered in this fashion. (Unfortunately, the survey in asking this question did not specify the wage offered, that is, whether it was the day-shift

TABLE 30
Shift Differentials, 1927 and 1937
(percent)

	Differential of Firms Paying	Percent Paying	Differential of All Firms Working Shifts
1927	11.4	33	3.7
1937	7.0	29	2.0

Sources: Calculations by author based on National Industrial Conference Board data.

wage or the day-shift wage plus the premium reported. As long as the questions were the same in both years, a comparison should be valid.)

The next question is whether these NICB surveys can be used in combination with the BLS material; if so, we have a long time series—of sorts—going back to the 1920s. The NICB data apparently refer to big firms, considerably larger than average firms in industry. When I examined the size of wage differentials paid by three sizes of plants for a recent year, I found that in manufacturing the largest plants paid differentials that were 21 percent and 22 percent greater than industry average differentials.[25] Consequently I multiplied the raw 1927 and 1937 results by 0.823 (=1 ÷ 1.215) to make a crude level correction. These are the figures that appear in table 31 for those two years.

If these figures, particularly those before 1959, are valid, we find the following: as shown in table 31, the late-shift differential in manufacturing in relation to straight-time wages rose—apart from the depression—from 1927 to the early postwar period and thereafter to the late 1950s. This rise reflected a growing proportion of firms that paid a differential, which offset a decline in the percentage differential. By 1959, however, a very high proportion of those on shift work got a differential. Consequently the dominant influence after 1959 was the continuing decline in the percentage differential. Thus the rising wage differential may have been a factor inhibiting the spread of shift work from the end of World War II to 1959 or so. Here the WLB decision seems to have been of some importance although, given the experience in World War II and the growth of trade unionism, it seems unlikely that many firms could ever again attract labor to work at night in a high-employment economy without some inducement in the form of higher wages. After 1959 the relative decline in the percentage wage differential probably fostered the growth of shift work.[26]

TABLE 31

WAGE DIFFERENTIALS FOR LATE SHIFTS IN MANUFACTURING AS
PERCENTAGE OF STRAIGHT-TIME HOURLY EARNINGS, 1927–1979
(percent)

	Differential of Firms Paying	Percent Paying	Differential of All Firms Working Shifts
1927	11.4	33	3.0
1937	7.0	29	1.7
1945–46	6.4	57	3.6
1959–60	5.1	94	4.8
1969	4.5	99	4.5
1979	4.0	99	4.0

NOTE: Data from 1959 forward refer to second shift. Data for 1945–46 refer to second shift and "general night work" differential. Data for 1927 and 1937 refer to "general night" differential and second shift.

SOURCES: See tables 29 and 30 and note 24. Data for 1969 and 1979 are from BLS, *Area Wage Surveys, Metropolitan Areas, United States and Regional Summaries, 1969–70*, Bulletin 1660–92, and similar unpublished data for 1979. All calculations are by author based on BLS and NICB data.

Technological Developments. According to Philip S. Schmidt,[27] the development of electric lighting early in this century permitted the introduction of multiple shifts in factories. This could well have been important in the early growth of shift work. The growth of the automobile may also have been important in increasing the labor supply available for evening and night work.

Regressions

Some of the preceding discussion and the data used in support of various hypotheses suggest the possibility of a model to describe the factors influencing shift work. The model says that average weekly plant hours have increased in response to an increase in the capital intensity of production, as measured by the ratio of capital to labor, but that wage premiums at first hampered and then encouraged the spread of late-shift work. At least two other related influences also appear to be of importance: the growth of manufacturing capital in the South, the influence of which is positive, and the share of value added accounted for by single-unit firms, the influence of which is negative.

Where data were not available for specific years, they were obtained by straight-line interpolation. They are shown in appendix I, table 56, for the period 1948–1976.

Although I did some experimentation with the data for the longer time period—1929–1976—I did not pursue it. Ideally I would have compared a 1929–1948 equation with one for the 1948–1976 period, but in view of the data limitations for the pre–World War II period, I did not think the effort was warranted. Furthermore, the depression years pose a serious problem. This study is one of long-term trends, and the 1930s raise the question of how to adjust a variable like the capital-labor ratio to reflect high-employment conditions. The apparent adjustments are so large that one may seriously question their validity. Consequently the analysis presented here is confined to postwar years.

Finally, in the choice of the dependent variable, should one analyze all manufacturing or what has been labeled "all-other" manufacturing, that is, the manufacturing total excluding no-shift and continuous industries? Both types of analysis were tried, but better results were obtained using average weekly plant hours in the all-other manufacturing group as the dependent variable.

Results of the analysis are given below following a discussion of some data problems.

Capital-Labor Ratio. This is a more refined measure than the one discussed in the section on capital intensity. Appendix G describes the derivation of this series except for one adjustment: the labor figures are seriously affected by the business cycle. Consequently an adjustment was made so that labor is on a potential basis; this requires an adjustment to labor input in each year that the unemployment rate deviates from 4 percent.[28] One can criticize the use of 4 percent as a standard for potential, particularly since manufacturing employment is more cyclically volatile than employment for the economy as a whole. The adjustment should be helpful, but it should be viewed as rough in the absence of a careful investigation.

Wage Differential. The data in table 31 were used to make interpolations for the years between 1945 and 1959. Annual data from 1959 onward were available from BLS sources (see figure 2).

Share of Capital in the South. The years from 1929 to 1962 are based on census horsepower figures for 1929, 1939, 1954, and 1962. With 1962 as a link, I then used the share of gross fixed assets (based on historical cost) accounted for by the southern states as shown in census data. Breakdowns by state of gross fixed assets were available for each year in the following periods: 1962–1964, 1967–1971, 1974–1977. Other years were based on straight-line interpolation.

Share of Value Added in Single-Unit Firms. See table 27 for benchmarks from census. Intervening years were based on straight-line interpolation.

Regression Results. Several forms of the relation were tried, but the best results seemed to be simple linear forms. For the two independent variables whose theoretical basis is strongest we have

$$Average\ weekly\ plant\ hours\ (AWPH) = \underset{(26.0)}{113.2} + \underset{(19.6)}{.82\ KL} - \underset{(2.4)}{2.4\ WD} \qquad (2)$$

where KL is the capital-labor ratio with labor adjusted for deviations from 4 percent unemployment and WD is the wage differential.

For equation 2, $R^2 = .932$; t-statistics are shown in parentheses.

The addition of variables measuring the share of capital in the South and the percentage of output accounted for by single-unit firms yielded disappointing results in terms of regression coefficients. These two variables and the capital-labor ratio are all highly correlated with one another, and it is impossible to measure the separate influence of each in the same equation.

Notes

1. Charles O'Connor, "Late Shift Employment in Manufacturing Industries," *Monthly Labor Review* (November 1970), p. 37. See also Roger R. Betancourt and Christopher K. Clague, "An Econometric Analysis of Capital Utilization," *International Economic Review*, vol. 19 (February 1978), pp. 211–27.

2. Bureau of Labor Statistics, U.S. Department of Labor, *Supplementary Wage Practices in American Industry, 1945/46*, Bulletin 939 (1948), pp. 1–2.

3. This refers to the basic tabulation for 1929 that was used in the first study. See Murray F. Foss, *Changes in the Workweek of Fixed Capital: U.S. Manufacturing, 1929 to 1976* (Washington, D.C.: American Enterprise Institute, 1981), esp. app. D.

4. Ibid., p. 70.

5. National Industrial Conference Board, *Studies in Personnel Policy, No. 3: Multiple-Shift Operation* (New York: NICB, 1937). When long-term comparisons are made, the years being compared should be about the same stage of the business cycle. It is hard to evaluate October 1937 in relation to 1929. The Federal Reserve Board's index of industrial production (seasonally adjusted) in October 1937 was 2.6 percent below the 1929 average (Federal Reserve Board, *Industrial Production 1957–59 Base*, 1962). Use of shift work in 1937 may have been a little low on this account.

6. National Industrial Conference Board, *Night Work in Industry* (New York: NICB, 1927). The entire sample, covering manufacturing and nonmanufacturing, was based on reports from 243 companies with 1,175,000 employees.

7. The survey covered "plants with varying size located in different sections of the country and manufacturing a wide variety of products." Ibid., p. 3.

8. See Murray F. Foss, "The Utilization of Capital Equipment," *Survey of Current Business*, vol. 43 (June 1963), pp. 8–16.

9. August–December 1945, that is, average pertains to the months after the end of the war. Source: table 21.

10. Referring to a study as of April 1937, A. F. Hinrichs wrote: "The second shift has in fact become all but universal. . . . only 2 out of 186 mills in the South and 14 out of 58 plants in the North were on 1 shift. But . . . there was evidence of a substantial third-shift operation." BLS, *Wages in Cotton-Goods Manufacturing*, Bulletin 662 (November 1938), p. 27.

11. Paul Taubman and Peter Gottschalk raised questions about the representativeness of the SMSAs in "The Average Workweek of Capital in Manufacturing," *Journal of the American Statistical Association*, vol. 66, no. 335 (September 1971), pp. 448–55.

12. John W. Kendrick, *Productivity Trends in the United States* (Princeton, N.J.: Princeton University Press, 1961), p. 464.

13. For industry detail supporting the same point, see Foss, *Changes in the Workweek of Fixed Capital*, table 35, pp. 96–98.

14. Robin Marris had called attention to this in *The Economics of Capital Utilization* (Cambridge: Cambridge University Press, 1964).

15. Foss, *Changes in the Workweek of Fixed Capital*, pp. 44–52.

16. Actually the comparison was between 1929 and 1976 rather than between, say, 1937 and, say, 1941. See ibid., pp. 48–49.

17. Wage differentials for second and third shifts appear in BLS Area Wage Survey summaries. Basic data pertaining to shift differentials usually had to be combined by the author into averages. These statistics appear in BLS, *Area Wage Surveys, Metropolitan Areas, United States and Regional Summaries*, various issues. For 1977, for example, see the volume published as Bulletin 1950-77, October 1980, p. 103. Average differentials were then expressed as percentages of average hourly Earnings excluding overtime in manufacturing (BLS, *Employment and Earnings, United States, 1909–78*, Bulletin 1312-11, 1979, p. 930).

18. This was pointed out by O'Connor, "Late Shift Employment in Manufacturing Industries," p. 41.

19. Foss, *Changes in the Workweek of Fixed Capital*, p. 42.

20. The 57 percent is not weighted by employment and consequently may be too low to the extent that larger firms working shifts were more likely to pay a differential than smaller firms.

21. "Pay Differentials for Night Work under Union Agreements," *Monthly Labor Review* (July 1943), p. 134; Morton Levine and James Nix, "Shift Operations and Differentials in Union Contracts, 1952," *Monthly Labor Review* (November 1952), p. 496; BLS, *Premium Pay for Night, Weekend and Overtime Work in*

Union Contracts, Bulletin 1251 (1958), p. 2.

22. Basic Steel Case, November 25, 1944. Director and Office of Economic Stabilization, Directives of March 8, 1945, and April 24, 1945. See National War Labor Board, *Termination Report,* pp. 355–59.

23. Under the rotating shift system (common in continuous industries) workers take turns working daytime, evening, and night shifts.

24. National Industrial Conference Board, *Night Work in Industry,* and *Studies in Personnel Policy No. 3.*

25. See BLS, *Area Wage Surveys, Metropolitan Areas, United States and Regional Summaries, 1977,* Bulletin 1950–77, p. 99.

26. I speculated about reasons for the decline in the wage differential in my first study. See Foss, *Changes in the Workweek of Fixed Capital,* pp. 49–51, 56.

27. Philip S. Schmidt, "The Form Value of Electricity: Some Observations and Cases," Electric Power Research Institute, Workshop on Electricity Use, Productive Efficiency and Economic Growth, Washington, D.C., December 8–9, 1983, p. 1.

28. In his analyses of growth Denison adjusts total factor productivity each year for variations in the intensity of demand. My specific adjustment is different, however. See Edward F. Denison, *Accounting for United States Economic Growth, 1929–1969* (Washington, D.C.: Brookings Institution, 1974), pp. 66–67.

4
Nonmanufacturing Industries

Outside of manufacturing, industries in the nonfarm business sector can be divided into two groups for purposes of this study: those whose capital is available and operates throughout the day and year, like the electric and gas utilities, and all others. The dichotomy is useful because the former group has experienced no change in average weekly hours of operation and because in terms of gross stocks of fixed capital it accounts for more than two-fifths of the weight of the nonfarm business sector. As for the other industries, generalizing about them is difficult except to say that the principles governing the adoption of shift work found in manufacturing should operate here. The force of custom or consumer habits, however, is more important in industries like retail trade than in manufacturing. Basic data come from a variety of sources. The study makes use of some BLS Industry Wage Surveys for coal mining; a small survey of retail-store hours gleaned from newspaper ads going back to 1929; a special tabulation of weekly hours worked by proprietors from the decennial censuses of 1950, 1960, and 1970 supplemented with similar information from the 1977 Current Population Survey; and a tabulation of broadcasting hours by television and radio stations. In the absence of statistical information I had to resort to assumptions about some industries, like construction, in which shift work is quite uncommon and average weekly capital hours are assumed to move like average weekly hours of labor.

This chapter provides a brief description of the continuous nonmanufacturing industries followed by a discussion of mining, focusing mainly on coal. After that comes a discussion of retail trade. Notes concerning detailed kinds of business in retail trade are listed in Appendix B. Appendix C covers wholesale trade; D, services; and E, construction, finance, and communications except telephones.

Continuous Nonmanufacturing Industries

Table 32 shows the industries included in the continuous nonmanufacturing group and their importance in relation to the total gross

TABLE 32

REAL GROSS CAPITAL STOCKS OF CONTINUOUS NONMANUFACTURING
INDUSTRIES AS PERCENTAGE OF TOTAL NONFARM BUSINESS STOCKS,
1948 AND 1973
(percent)

	1948	1973
Crude petroleum and natural gas	7.8	5.4
Transportation	23.9	12.4
Railroads	17.5	6.6
Electric, gas, and water utilities	12.6	15.0
Communication except broadcasting	3.8	6.9
Hotels and motels	3.9	2.5
Hospitals (for profit)	0.2	0.4
Total	52.2	42.6
Total excluding railroads	34.7	36.0

NOTE: Based on stocks in 1972 dollars. Excludes nonprofit organizations including hospitals.

SOURCE: Author, mainly on the basis of BLS data: *Capital Stock Estimates for Input-Output Industries*, BLS Bulletin 2034 (1979).

stock of nonfarm business fixed capital. Two points about the transportation division may be noted. First, strictly speaking, local transportation is not a continuous industry since bus lines are ordinarily closed in the early morning hours. Airlines may also operate less than a full day. I did not think this a serious misclassification, however, since the *change* in scheduled hours has probably been quite small. Second, although the railroads run at all hours of the day and night, this does not necessarily mean that the capital is never idle. Freight cars are said to work only a small part of a twenty-four-hour day; but that kind of "efficiency" is not being measured in this study (see chapter 1, "Two Kinds of Changes in Capital Hours"). The reader should also keep in mind that the exclusion of the nonprofit sector means excluding most hospitals and that residential capital such as apartment houses is also not included.

From 1948 to 1973 the continuous nonmanufacturing group as a whole declined in relative importance, but if railroads are excluded the group shows a small increase. Table 33 gives an annual time series of the relative importance of the continuous group, including and excluding railroads.

TABLE 33

GROSS CAPITAL STOCKS OF CONTINUOUS NONMANUFACTURING
INDUSTRIES AS PERCENTAGE OF TOTAL NONFARM STOCKS, 1947–1974
(percent)

	All Nonfarm Business	Nonfarm Business Excluding Railroads
1947	52.7	34.7
1948	52.2	34.7
1949	52.1	34.8
1950	51.8	35.0
1951	51.3	35.0
1952	51.2	35.3
1953	51.1	35.6
1954	50.6	35.7
1955	50.1	35.7
1956	49.4	35.6
1957	49.0	35.7
1958	48.8	36.0
1959	48.5	36.2
1960	48.2	36.3
1961	47.9	36.4
1962	47.5	36.4
1963	47.0	36.4
1964	46.5	36.3
1965	45.8	36.0
1966	45.0	35.6
1967	44.5	35.5
1968	44.1	35.6
1969	43.6	35.5
1970	43.4	35.7
1971	43.3	35.9
1972	42.9	35.9
1973	42.6	36.0
1974	42.4	36.1

NOTE: Based on stocks in 1972 dollars.

SOURCE: Author, mainly on the basis of BLS data: *Capital Stock Estimates for Input-Output Industries*, BLS Bulletin 2034 (1979), app. C.

Mining

Mining is dominated by the crude petroleum and natural gas industry, which operates continuously and, in 1974, accounted for almost three-quarters of gross stocks of fixed capital in mining. Our problem is to develop time series on hours worked by capital in mining industries other than crude petroleum and natural gas. Most of the discussion presented here concerns coal.

Coal. Average weekly hours worked by coal mines increased 43 percent from 1929 to 1976, and the rise since 1948 is estimated to be 28 percent. The increase reflects two main influences. First, there has been a shift in output from underground to surface mines, a change that has meant a shift toward more capital-intensive methods. In 1929 surface mining accounted for 3.3 percent of physical output; by 1976 this proportion had risen to 56.6 percent. Second, underground mining itself has become more capital intensive. Changes in production methods for the industry as a whole have been dramatic since the early postwar period, as the following figures suggest:[1]

	Production	Production Worker Employment	Weekly Hours of Labor	Gross Stock of Fixed Capital
1948	100	100	100	100
1976	113	45	106	336 (1974)

Underground mines. Trends in the proportions of workers employed on late shifts in underground mines are illustrated in the left-hand side of table 34, which relies on Industry Wage Surveys conducted by the BLS and data on employment by shift published in the 1939 Census of Mineral Industries. The increase in the proportions on late shifts is striking. The inclusion of 1939 in such a comparison might be questioned since 1939, when bituminous coal production was 27 percent below its 1929 level, was a depressed year generally. Demand and output were strong in 1944, a wartime year, however; since then the proportion of workers on late shifts has risen by 87 percent.

The increase in late-shift employment evident in table 34 seems to be associated with the increased capital intensity of coal mining and the spread of continuous mining machinery. Cutting coal by machine instead of by hand was a relatively early mining innovation that by 1929 accounted for 78 percent of underground bituminous output. By the late 1940s this early equipment gave way to continuous mining machines; in 1976 some 64 percent of underground production was

TABLE 34

Production Workers Employed on Late Shifts in Bituminous Coal Mining, 1939–1976

(percent)

	Underground			Surface		
	2d shift	3d shift	Total	2d shift	3d shift	Total
1939	18.9	2.6	21.5			
1944	23.4	3.6	27.0	16.0[a]	6.0	22.0
1962	30.3	10.6	40.9	21.9	9.9	31.8
1967	30.0	16.6	46.6			
1976[b]	31.5	19.1	50.6			

a. 1945.
b. Includes 1977.
Sources: 1944–1976: BLS Industry Wage Surveys. 1939: Bureau of the Census, *Census of Mineral Industries*, table 19, p. 86.

mined with continuous equipment. Other innovation also spread. Mechanical loading of coal, applicable to surface as well as to underground mines, grew steadily after its introduction in the early 1920s and by 1954 accounted for 84 percent of output.

Shift work was used in 1929, but direct information on its relative importance is not available. In a 1930 study the BLS noted that its survey of wages and hours was limited to day workers and that reports were received from "a number of mines in which machine miners work at night."[2] In the Census of Mines and Quarries for 1929, the census questionnaire contains questions (item 4, General Schedule) asking for the normal number of hours the plant (mine) was operated per day and per week, as well as for the number of shifts operated per day. (These are the same questions asked of manufacturers whose answers I used to measure manufacturing plant hours in 1929 in *Changes in the Workweek of Fixed Capital*.) A search by the Bureau of the Census, however, failed to turn up either the schedules or a microfilm of them. We do know that in bituminous coal mining the normal workweek for *labor* in 1929 was forty-eight hours, reflecting a six-day week of eight hours per day. The eight-hour day for labor had been in effect since April 1898.[3]

If 27.0 percent of workers were employed on late shifts in 1944, which reflected operations under wartime demand, using the 1939 shift pattern—21.5 percent—as an indication of the 1929 pattern did not seem entirely unreasonable. This gives us three years—1929, 1944, and 1976—as points on a long-term trend line (see table 35). Intervening years were obtained by interpolation. To measure capital hours, however, it is also necessary to allow for the fact that more hours per shift and days per week were worked in 1929 than in 1939.

I hesitated to use the manufacturing equation relating the proportion of employment on late shifts to average weekly plant hours because mining technology is quite different from manufacturing technology. Consequently I assumed that the distribution of employment by shift was a reasonable indicator of capital utilization by shift. This is a simplifying but not a bad assumption if it is used with some care, and it seems to be appropriate for underground coal mining.[4] That assumption presupposes that all workers work with fixed capital of some kind, that the ratio of operating fixed capital per worker is unchanged across the shifts, and that all the available capital is used on the first shift. One difficulty is that we know that some workers are engaged in maintenance, which is often concentrated on the first shift.

According to table 35, 19.1 percent of production workers in 1976 worked on the third shift. This then is the weight for capital operating three shifts. Capital operating two shifts but not three would have a weight of 12.4 since, of the 31.5 percent shown on the second shift, 19.1 percent operated both a second and a third shift. Finally, the capital operating a single shift is represented by the remainder: the first-shift proportion less the other two, or 49.4 − 12.4 − 19.1 = 17.9. These are the 1976 figures shown in table 36.

According to data on union contracts, the average labor shift—

TABLE 35

DISTRIBUTION OF EMPLOYMENT IN UNDERGROUND BITUMINOUS COAL MINING, BY SHIFT, 1929, 1944, AND 1976

(percent)

Shift	1929[a]	1944	1976
1st	78.5	73.0	49.4
2d	18.9	23.4	31.5
3d	2.6	3.6	19.1
Total	100.0	100.0	100.0

a. Distribution assumed to be the same as in 1939.
SOURCE: Table 34.

TABLE 36

ESTIMATED WEIGHTS FOR CAPITAL BY NUMBER OF SHIFTS PER
UNIT OF CAPITAL IN UNDERGROUND BITUMINOUS COAL MINING,
1929, 1944, AND 1976

	1929		1944		1976	
	Weight	%	Weight	%	Weight	%
3-shift capital	2.6	3.3	3.6	4.9	19.1	38.7
2-shift capital	16.3	20.7	19.8	27.1	12.4	25.1
1-shift capital	59.7	76.0	49.6	67.9	17.9	36.2
Total	78.5	100.0	73.0	100.0	49.4	100.0

NOTE: Detail may not add to totals because of rounding.
SOURCE: Calculations by author based on table 35.

including travel time—in bituminous coal in 1976 was 7.5 hours. This figure combined with the weights in table 36 yields an operating day of 15.18 hours. Assuming further an operating week of five days yields 75.9 hours per week for 1976. The 1944 and 1929 estimates were done in a similar fashion after making allowance for differences in hours per shift and days per week. The data used are shown in table 37.

Surface mines. The same technique used for underground mining did not seem to be appropriate for surface mining, which is highly capital intensive. Surface mining is often done with large draglines and shovels, which tend to be operated many hours per week, frequently around the clock, because of their high cost. In parts of the country, however, production is less capital intensive, and equipment is used fewer hours per week.

I have used a constant figure of 100 hours per week for capital engaged in surface production. With weights based on shares of production, I combined average weekly hours for underground coal with those for surface mining to derive the overall bituminous figure shown in table 38. The paragraphs that follow explain the derivation of the figure used for surface mining.

First, I obtained some rough ideas of equipment hours and weights for various types of equipment actually employed in a given surface operation.[5]

	Hours per Week	Weight
Draglines	140	15
Trucks	100	70
Front-end loaders	90	10
Scrapers	70	5
		100

On a weighted basis the figures above would yield an average of about 104 hours per week; but this figure would be far too high for Appalachian states, where the workweek of surface mines might be fifty hours. Fortunately I had some information by which I could differentiate among areas of the country. In its latest Industry Wage Survey of the bituminous coal industry, the BLS shows proportions of production workers on late shifts in surface mining for selected states.[6] These proportions with data on the production of bituminous coal in surface mines in 1976 are shown in table 39, in which states have been grouped into three classes reflecting high, medium, and low proportions of employment on late shifts.

On the basis of the information cited above, I assumed that the

TABLE 37

HOURS FOR LABOR AND MINE OPERATION IN UNDERGROUND
BITUMINOUS COAL MINING, 1929, 1944, AND 1976

	Hours per Labor Shift	Mine Hours per Day	Mine Days per Week	Mine Hours per Week[a]
1929	8.0	10.18	6.000	61.1
1944	8.0	10.96	5.375	58.9
1976	7.5	15.18	5.000	75.9

a. Mine hours per week: column 2 times column 3.

SOURCES: Mine hours per day are based on table 36 and hours per labor shift. Hours per labor shift: 1929: Wolman, *Hours of Work*, p. 3. 1944: BLS, *Wage Chronology: Bituminous Coal Mine Operators and United Mine Workers of America, October 1933–November 1974*, Bulletin 1799 (1973), p. 11; refers to daily hours of work by inside day workers. 1976: BLS, *Supplement to Wage Chronology Bulletin 1799* (1977), p. 3; refers to daily hours paid for work in underground deep mines. Mine days per week: 1929: Wolman, *Hours of Work*, p. 3. 1944: average weekly hours in bituminous coal were 43.0 in 1944 (BLS, *Employment and Earnings, United States, 1909–78*, Bulletin 1312–11), p. 21; this figure was divided by eight hours per shift to yield days per week. 1976: a five-day week was worked by 93 percent of inside workers in underground mines in January 1976 (BLS, *Industry Wage Survey*, Bulletin 1999, p. 21).

TABLE 38

AVERAGE WEEKLY HOURS OPERATED BY FIXED CAPITAL IN BITUMINOUS
COAL MINING, 1929–1976

	1929	1948	1959	1976
Underground mines				
Hours	61.1	60.9	66.4	75.9
Weight	96.2	76.7	68.8	43.4
Surface mines				
Hours	———assumed constant at 100 hours———			
Weight	3.8	23.3	31.2	56.6
All operations				
Hours	62.6	70.0	76.9	89.5

SOURCE: Author. Productivity weights derived from National Coal Association, *Coal Facts 1978–79* (Washington, D.C., no date).

high-shift states work 120 hours, the medium-shift work 80 hours, and the low-shift work 50 hours. These weekly hours were subject to two sets of weights: the volume of surface production and a capital factor. The weights of 120, 80, and 50 assumed above do not reflect the possibility that capital requirements per unit of output for the mines working the longest hours might be double those of the middle group according to William Hynan of the National Coal Association. I accepted this ratio and arbitrarily set the weight for the low group at one-half the middle group. This yields a weighted average of 107 hours per week, which I arbitrarily rounded down to 100.

Proportion of Employment on Late Shifts	Production Weight	Capital Factor	Adjusted Production Weight	Weekly Hours
High	179.3	2	358.6	120
Medium	30.0	1	30.0	80
Low	132.6	1/2	66.3	50
			454.9	(107.2)

I had no information about the change in weekly hours but assumed it was approximately constant over the entire period, given its high level. Summary figures are given in table 38.

Other Minerals. Other industries in mining were estimated by the same general method used to estimate weekly hours operated by

TABLE 39

PERCENTAGE OF WORKERS ON LATE SHIFTS AND NET SURFACE
PRODUCTION IN BITUMINOUS COAL MINING, SELECTED STATES, 1976

	Workers on Late Shifts[a] (%)	Net Surface Production (millions of tons)	Assumed Weekly Hours of Operation
High-Shift Operations			
Illinois	50.1	27.2	
Kentucky (West)	47.7	28.9	
Mountain states	45.8	87.2	
Indiana[b]	NA	24.9	
North Dakota[c]	NA	11.1	
Total		179.3	120
Medium-Shift Operations			
Ohio	32.5	30.0	80
Low-Shift Operations			
Pennsylvania	20.3	42.0	
Kentucky (East)	14.3	50.6	
West Virginia	15.9	21.3	
Virginia	NA	13.9	
Tennessee	NA	4.8	
Total		132.6	50
Total of states specified		341.9	
Total of U.S. surface production		383.9	

NA = Not applicable.
a. January 1976.
b. Suggested classification by William Hynan of the National Coal Association.
c. Classification by author.

SOURCES: BLS, *Industry Wage Survey: Bituminous Coal, January 1976–March 1981,* Bulletin 1999 (1978), p. 45. Production from National Coal Association, *Coal Facts 1978–79,* p. 81.

underground coal mines. The industry detail in which the calculations were made was governed by the availability of BLS industry data on employment by shift for World War II and some recent year. Because 1929 statistics pertaining to employment by shift were not available, the assumption was made that the distribution of employment by shift was the same in 1929 as in 1939, for which year census data were available. As in underground coal mining, however, the length of a labor shift and the number of days worked per week were greater in 1929 than in 1939.

Iron ore. For iron ore we have two Industry Wage Surveys—one for 1943 and another for 1976–1977—showing the proportion of workers on late shifts, plus similar information from the 1939 Census of Mines (see table 40).

I decided not to use the 1939 figures with a five-day, forty-hour labor week for 1929 because doing so would have yielded a figure for capital hours that was cyclically low. Iron ore production in 1939, for example, was 20 percent below the average level in the 1926–1930 period. I assumed that there was little change in plant hours between 1929 and 1943, which would be close to the result of assuming a six-day, forty-eight-hour labor week. On the assumption that capital hours were proportional to labor hours, as described in the preceding pages for underground bituminous coal, I obtained the following average weekly plant hours:

1929	68.3
1943	64.5
1976–1977	67.4

Intervening years were obtained by straight-line interpolation.

Nonferrous metals. For metals other than iron I had 1977 figures for employment by shift for copper, for lead and zinc, and for uranium, vanadium, and radium. Figures for several types of nonferrous metals combined were available for 1943, and separate figures were available from the 1939 census (see table 41). As with iron ore, I used the shift data from 1939 and a six-day workweek to get figures for 1929.

This calculation yielded estimates of average weekly plant hours as shown in table 42. The three groups were combined with horse-

---

TABLE 40

DISTRIBUTION OF EMPLOYMENT IN IRON ORE MINING, BY SHIFT, 1939, 1943, AND 1976–1977

(percent)

	Shift			
	1st	2d	3d	Total
1939	70.3	26.9	2.8	100.0
1943	62.0	23.0	15.0	100.0
1976–77	59.3	20.8	19.9	100.0

SOURCES: BLS Bulletins 787 (1944), and 2017 (1979), p. 8; and 1939 Census of Mineral Industries, table 19, pp. 86–87.

82

TABLE 41

DISTRIBUTION OF EMPLOYMENT IN NONFERROUS METAL MINING,
BY SHIFT, 1939, 1943, AND 1977

(percent)

| | Shift | | | |
	1st	2d	3d	Total
	Copper			
1939	65.8	27.0	7.2	100.0
1943[a]	65.0	25.0	10.0	100.0
1977	58.8	21.9	19.3	100.0
	Lead and Zinc			
1939	71.8	22.4	5.8	100.0
1943[a]	65.0	25.0	10.0	100.0
1977	59.2	29.5	11.3	100.0
	Uranium, Vanadium, and Radium			
1939	96.3	1.9	1.8	100.0
1943[a]	65.0	25.0	10.0	100.0
1977	58.1	26.7	15.2	100.0

a. In 1943 the BLS published only *combined* results for copper, lead, zinc, mercury, bauxite, molybdenum, tungsten, and manganese.

SOURCES: BLS Bulletins 765 (1943) and 2017 (1979), pp. 11–27; and 1939 Census of Mineral Industries, table 19, pp. 86–87.

TABLE 42

AVERAGE WEEKLY PLANT HOURS IN METAL MINING,
1929, 1943, AND 1977

	1929	1943	1977
Copper	72.9	61.6	68.3
Lead and zinc	66.8	61.6	69.2
Uranium[a]	49.8	61.6	69.7
Weighted average	69.8	61.6	68.8

a. Includes vanadium and radium ore.

SOURCE: See text.

power weights from the census. Average 1929–1939 weights were used for the years 1929–1939; average 1939–1954 weights were used for the years 1940–1954; and 1954 weights were used for the years 1955–1976. Other years were obtained by interpolation.

Stone, clay, and sand. In contrast with the mining discussed thus far, I decided to accept the average weekly plant hours derived from the 1939 census because these industries engage in very little shift work. This calculation yielded a figure of 45.8 hours for 1939. For 1929 I assumed a six-day week, which gave 55.0 hours. For 1977 I used a distribution of employment by shift from a special tabulation of the Current Population Survey for March 1977 to obtain a figure of 48.8 hours per week.

Thus this industry experienced a fairly substantial drop in weekly capital hours from 1929 to 1939 but a slight rise from 1939 to 1976. Intervening years were obtained by interpolation.

Retail Trade

For the most part retail stores maintain store hours to suit the desires of their customers. And in the past they have responded with little delay to the changed shopping habits of consumers. The competitive nature of the retail industry would operate in this direction since otherwise a store could increase its market share by offering more service than its competitors in the form of longer store hours.[7] In 1940 and 1941, when retail sales began to respond to rising incomes that in turn reflected the step-up in national defense activity, a number of stores began to provide nighttime shopping hours. This was to accommodate the needs of defense workers, many of whom were engaged in overtime work that often included Saturdays. But the trend to longer store hours began in earnest after the end of World War II, especially with the increased participation of women in the labor force. Longer hours became a feature of large stores in newly built suburban shopping centers. The trend to longer hours was reinforced by the repeal of blue laws, which had prohibited stores from remaining open on Sunday, and by a concomitant change in attitudes toward Sunday shopping on the part of the public. But it is also likely that the increased capital intensity of retail operations has been a factor leading to longer store hours.

Small stores either did not participate in this movement toward longer hours or at least were limited in their ability to do so. A plausible hypothesis, for which some support was found in manufacturing, is that the owner was unwilling either to lengthen for himself a workweek that was already long or to incur the added costs of, say, a manager because the added revenues would not warrant such costs.

The procedure in retail was to divide the industry division into several kinds of business (food, general merchandise, and so forth) and within each kind of business to divide sales between those of single-unit firms and those of multi-unit firms. These constituted weights within the kind of business. Sales data of this type have been collected by the Bureau of the Census in each Retail Trade Census since 1929 and are described below. Estimates of store hours were made for each kind of business, although it is important to emphasize that actual data were quite limited and a good deal of judgment had to be used to obtain the results shown here. For general merchandise and related stores I used small samples of stores for which it was possible to obtain weekly store hours from newspaper advertisements for selected years going back to 1929. Trends based on the averages shown by these samples were used for multi-unit stores and were often imputed to single-unit stores in the early years. From 1950 onward, however, I relied on statistics of hours worked by retail proprietors to estimate hours of small or single-unit stores. These statistics came from tabulations made especially for this study on the basis of the 1960 and 1970 population censuses and the March 1977 Current Population Survey, supplemented with data from the 1950 census.

To obtain an estimate of retail store hours for all kinds of business combined, hours by kind of business were weighted together on the basis of fixed weights. The book value of gross fixed assets I obtained from the 1972 Census of Business. I would have preferred weights from 1954, but 1972 was the first year such information became available from census sources.

On a combined basis retail store hours rose about 6 percent from 1948 to 1976 after having shown little change from 1929 to 1948. Retail indexes appear in table 1. Appendix B provides some detail for specific kinds of retail businesses.

Estimating Store Hours. I did not engage in an extensive search for store hours. Harold Barger cites a study made for a master's thesis at Columbia University in 1950 in which the author made estimates of average weekly labor hours in retail trade for the years 1880–1920.[8] This study gave a figure of sixty hours per week for hours worked by proprietors and unpaid family workers in 1919. Barger assumed that the figure of sixty hours was unchanged from 1919 to 1929 and 1939 (and apparently to 1949).

Use of newspaper advertisements. Daily newspapers were a source of information on store hours because stores have often shown their hours in newspaper advertisements. I took a sample of advertisements in eleven large cities for the first Thursday in May in 1929, 1940, 1950, 1960, 1970, and 1976. Any store that reported hours of operations for the week was recorded as an observation. Not all cities were available each year; and, of course, the composition of stores changed over the years. The number of stores varied from 49 in 1929 to 238 in 1976. For the most part the stores were department (general merchandise) stores, apparel stores, and furniture stores, or what the Bureau of the Census now refers to as the GAF group. The following is a list of the cities and the newspapers sampled.

City Sampled	Newspaper
Boston	Globe
New York	Daily News
Philadelphia	Bulletin
Washington	Post
Pittsburgh	Press
Chicago	Tribune
Detroit	News
St. Louis	Post Dispatch
Houston	Post
Los Angeles	Times
San Francisco	Chronicle

Obviously one cannot claim a great deal for the sampling method used, but I did not have the resources to attempt either a careful sampling plan or a larger list of cities. The main virtue of the figures is that they come from leading stores in leading cities and the dispersion around the averages was not great. I calculated several kinds of averages, but they yielded changes from 1929 to 1976 that fell into a rather narrow range, as table 43 indicates. I wound up using the figure shown on line 4 for the GAF group.

My guess is that this sample may have understated the rise in this group because the sample may be too heavily weighted with downtown stores and may not adequately reflect the large-scale move to the suburbs in the postwar period.

Hours worked by the self-employed. Hours worked by the self-employed were estimated from probability sample data taken from the population censuses of 1950, 1960, and 1970 and from the Current Population Survey for March 1977. The March 1977 figures were used to represent 1976.

The estimates are based on the experience of full-time workers. Full-time workers are defined as those working thirty-five hours per

TABLE 43

Average Weekly Hours of Operation, General Merchandise, Apparel, and Furniture Stores, 1929–1976

	1929	1940	1950	1960	1970	1976	% Change 1929–1976
1. Average of city averages	58.9	58.7	56.8	60.8	65.6	65.9	11.9
2. Average without regard to city	60.3	60.6	57.4	60.3	65.8	65.9	9.3
3. Sales weights for each year applied to (1)	58.3	56.5	55.9	58.4	63.0	64.5	10.6
4. Sales weights for each year applied to (2)	58.9	56.7	56.5	58.1	62.7	64.3	9.2
5. Fixed sales weights (1963) applied to (1)	58.5	58.7	57.2	61.3	65.0	65.9	12.6
6. 1963 weights applied to change of identical stores in adjacent years							9.0
Number of observations	49	78	196	221	236	238	

SOURCE: Tabulations by author. See text.

week or longer, but they do not constitute the universe of self-employed persons in this industry. In March 1977, for example, the number of the full-time self-employed was 78.4 percent of full-time plus part-time self-employed. Since the full-time self-employed worked an average of 47.7 hours per week, the implied hours for the part-time self-employed were 17.5 or the equivalent of 3.5 hours per day for five days. I decided to omit the part-time self-employed from my calculations because my interest is in a weekly store-hour figure weighted by capital. In terms of fixed capital the part-time self-employed would be greatly overweighted if represented by numbers of persons. Many of these part-time self-employed may be young persons whose main activity is going to school or semiretired persons who employ others full time at their place of business.

The 1960 and 1970 figures are mean weekly hours worked by full-time self-employed persons and are shown by kind of business in table 44. These figures were obtained in special tabulations made for this project by Dual Labs of Rosslyn, Virginia, on the basis of the 1–1,000 tapes available for public use. Since there were 1.2 million full-time persons in retail trade in 1970, the sampling ratio would yield approximately 1,200 persons. The 1976 figures came from a special tabulation made by the BLS from the Current Population Survey for March 1977. Because the 1960, 1970, and 1976 figures did not exhibit any particular trends, I accepted them as tabulated. For all retail self-employed combined, the figures show a slight dip from 1960 to 1970 and then a leveling (table 44, columns 4, 5, and 6).

To estimate 1950, I took the figures in column 4 for 1960 and moved them back by the 1950-to-1960 change in hours worked by self-employed managers, officials, and proprietors. These extrapolating series, which apply to persons working over thirty-four hours a week, come from data in the 1950 and 1960 population censuses. To use these it was necessary to combine men and women. Although the 1950 data are based on a $3^{1/3}$ percent sample and the 1960 data on a 5 percent sample and thus have smaller sampling errors than either the 1960 or the 1970 figures, I preferred the 1960–1970 set. The definitions in 1950 and 1960 are less clear-cut. They exclude persons who may have characterized themselves to census enumerators as self-employed "sales persons" rather than "proprietors" or "managers." In any case, the 1960 results from this source can be compared with the 1960 figures shown in column 4. The former tend to be a little higher for reasons that are not clear.

The final figures used for 1950 are given in column 1. Compared with 1960, 1970, and 1976 (columns 4, 5, and 6), the 1950 figure points

TABLE 44

Average Hours Worked by Full-Time Self-Employed Persons in Retail Trade, 1950–1976

	1950		1960		1970	1976
	(1)ᵃ	(2)	(3)	(4)	(5)	(6)
Lumber, building materials	55.0	56.4	55.9	54.5	52.4	56.4
General merchandise	57.3	59.9	56.8	54.3	53.7	51.7
Food	59.2	62.4	61.1	58.0	57.9	61.5
Motor vehicles	52.1	53.6	56.4	54.8	54.8	53.6
Gasoline	64.7	63.0	63.1	64.8	61.9	63.2
Apparel	45.0	47.1	51.6	49.3	49.7	45.6
Furniture and appliances	50.2	51.4	54.3	53.0	51.6	52.7
Eating and drinking	60.8	61.8	59.3	58.3	56.5	58.6
Drug }	55.3	56.0	54.8	59.2 54.1	55.1 54.5	55.9 52.9
All other }				53.5	54.0	52.7
Total retail	57.5	59.1	58.5	56.9	55.7	56.0

a. Adjusted 1950 figures: column 2 × column 4 ÷ column 3.

SOURCES: Column 2: 1950 Census. Column 3: 1960 Census Final Report, PC (2)-7A, Occupational Characteristics. Column 4: special tabulation from Dual Labs, 1960 Census. Column 5: special tabulation from Dual Labs, 1970 Census. Column 6: special tabulation from BLS, Current Population Survey (March 1977).

to a small decline in weekly hours of work over this twenty-six-year period.

Going back to 1929 from 1950 was in one sense easy because so little information was available. One of the interesting aspects of the figures in table 44 is their level: for the postwar period under consideration they seem to have remained rather high, at somewhat under sixty hours a week, and are far in excess of hours per week of labor. Full-time weekly hours of employees in retail trade were probably in the neighborhood of about forty in 1950. If proprietor hours were as high in 1950 as sixty per week, how much higher could they have been in 1929? I felt that it was entirely reasonable that store hours did not change much from 1929 to 1950, and as a consequence in a number of instances I assumed no change over this period. Barger also assumes an unchanged number of hours worked by proprietors from 1929 to 1948 at sixty hours per week.[9] John Kendrick, however, shows a pronounced decline in proprietor hours from 1929 to 1948 because the workweek of labor dropped considerably over this period and the workweek of proprietors was assumed to follow a similar trend.[10]

TABLE 45

RETAIL STORE SALES, 1929–1977

	All Stores ($ billions)	Single-Unit Firms ($ billions)	Single-Unit Firms as Percentage of All Stores
1929	49.1	33.7[a]	68.6
1935	32.8	21.3[a]	64.9
1939	42.0	27.4[a]	65.2
1948	130.5	91.8	70.3
1954	170.0	118.8	69.9
1958	199.6	132.4	66.3
1963	244.2	154.7	63.3
1967	310.2	186.7	60.2
1972[b]	447.1	245.2	54.8
1977[b]	710.0	369.3	52.0

a. Limited to independent stores; excludes utility-operated stores, state liquor stores, and mail-order stores.
b. Data reflect firms in business at year end.
SOURCES: 1929: 15th Census of the United States: 1930 Distribution, vol. 1, Retail Distribution, part 1, p. 68. 1929–1939: 16th Census of the United States: 1940 Census of Business, vol. 1, Retail Trade 1939, part 1, p. 69. 1948–1963: 1963 Census of Business, vol. 1, Retail Trade Summary Statistics, part 1. 1967–1977: Census of Retail Trade, vol. 1.

Kendrick includes part-time proprietors in his series, and I do not. But it is hard to see why the hours of proprietors should have dropped over this period, particularly since the hours of large stores were almost unchanged so far as one can tell from available information. Furthermore, proprietors might have competed with larger stores by offering more service in the form of longer hours per week. Finally, proprietors were not subject to the provisions of the Wage-Hour Law or the National Recovery Act so far as their own labor input was concerned.

Single- versus Multi-Unit Establishments. A fundamental breakdown used in retail trade for weighting purposes was the breakdown of sales between single and multi-unit stores within each kind of business. This information has been collected in each Census of Retail Trade with only small variations in the definitions used. Ratios for noncensus years were obtained by interpolation within each kind of business. The calculations would have been more consistent if fixed asset weights rather than sales weights had been employed, but this kind of information was not available.

The data for all retail trade are given in table 45. The importance of single-unit stores showed some decline in the 1930s, but the boom in new businesses by veterans after World War II reversed the trend. Some step-up in the rate of decrease seems to have occurred from 1963 to 1977.

Notes

1. The sources for the data are the following: production, Department of Energy; employment and hours, Bureau of Labor Statistics; capital, Bureau of Labor Statistics and Department of Commerce.

2. Bureau of Labor Statistics, U.S. Department of Labor, *Hours and Earnings in Bituminous Coal Mining*, Bulletin 516 (May 1939), p. 6.

3. Leo Wolman, *Hours of Work in American Industry* (New York: National Bureau of Economic Research, 1938), p. 3. Actual hours in 1929 were 38.1 because of depressed conditions in the industry.

4. See Murray F. Foss, "The Utilization of Capital Equipment," *Survey of Current Business*, vol. 43 (June 1963), p. 16. See also Paul Taubman and Peter Gottschalk, "The Average Workweek of Capital in Manufacturing," *Journal of the American Statistical Association*, vol. 66, no. 335 (September 1971), pp. 448–55.

5. I am indebted to William Hynan of the National Coal Association for these estimates.

6. BLS, *Industry Wage Survey: Bituminous Coal, Jan. 1976–March 1981*, Bulletin 1999 (1978), p. 45.

7. Exceptions, of course, are not hard to find. For example, in Detroit retail unions were apparently strong enough to keep automobile dealers from staying open on Saturdays, despite the depressed demand for automobiles in early 1982. Douglas R. Sears, "Detroit Car Dealers Debate Bright Ideas: Saturday Openings," *Wall Street Journal* (March 12, 1982).

8. Roselyn Silverman, "Hours Worked in Retail Trade, 1880–1920" (M.A. thesis, Columbia University, 1950). Averages by kind of business were weighted by number of retailers. Cited in Harold Barger, *Distribution's Place in the American Economy since 1869* (Princeton, N.J.: Princeton University Press for the National Bureau of Economic Research, 1955), pp. 11–12.

9. Barger, *Distribution's Place in the American Economy*.

10. John W. Kendrick, *Productivity Trends in the United States* (Princeton, N.J.: Princeton University Press for National Bureau of Economic Research, 1961), p. 491.

5
Office Equipment and Computers

Large mainframe computers operate very long hours and are substitutes for conventional office equipment that used to work forty hours a week for the most part. That the statistical procedures used thus far in this study have captured this development is most unlikely, and yet taking account of it in some fashion seems sensible. A service industry that sells computer services of various kinds exists, but computing is not an "industry" as that term has been used. I have constructed a synthetic industry, which could be called the office equipment industry, the capital of which consists of all the privately owned conventional office equipment plus all the privately owned computers in use. Because the computers have constituted an increasing share of this industry total, the average weekly capital hours worked by this synthetic group have shown a substantial increase over the period covered, although the weight of this group, while increasing, is still small. The existence of this synthetic industry, the capital of which is to be found in all conventionally defined industries using computers and office equipment, made it necessary to remove from all conventionally defined industries the estimated value of privately owned computers and other office equipment to avoid double counting in deriving an hours series for the private nonfarm business economy.

Hours Worked by Computers

My estimates of hours worked by computers are based on reports filed by federal agencies with the General Services Administration (GSA). For many years government agencies have been required to report a broad range of information concerning computer operations. Federal agencies were among the earliest users of computers, the adoption of which was encouraged by Congress as a means of reducing operating costs of government agencies. Today computers are found throughout the federal establishment performing a huge variety of tasks. At the same time, however, Congress has been aware of the possibilities of abuse and has required agencies like the Office of Management and Budget and the GSA to establish criteria for the purchase and rental of computers by the agencies. Because of this requirement and because of the widespread use of computers in the government, I felt that a series on hours worked by computers from government sources would be a reasonable proxy for a series based on the experience of computer use in private businesses, even though the government experience lacks the discipline of market forces. I was able to check certain figures on hours operated by computers in the federal government with data from private sector sources; this checking gave me a measure of confidence in what I had done.

The GSA has summarized data on the operating experience of computers in the "general management" classification in the federal government. General management refers to computers designed for general rather than highly specialized use, and as a consequence most of the computers used by the Department of Defense are excluded from the reports. A sample of these reports is given in table 46 for fiscal year 1977.

The figures actually reported by GSA are given in the stub and columns 2 and 4. The main point illustrated by this table is that the costlier the system, the longer the scheduled monthly hours of operation. The largest systems, those more than $1,500,000 per system, are operated on a schedule of 554 hours per month or 129 hours a week on the basis of 4.3 weeks per month. For the present stock of computers actual hours are a little below scheduled hours because of time out for maintenance, breakdowns, and so forth. For this study the concept of *scheduled* hours is the appropriate one.

To obtain weighted average hours, the number of systems shown in column 2 was multiplied by average price—which reflects my judgment within the limits of the class interval—to yield a value weight (column 3) that was applied to the hours figure for each class interval. The computers that run the longest hours per month account for only one-sixth of the number of systems but almost 60 percent of the total weight in terms of value.

Information of the kind illustrated in table 46 was available from GSA for the years 1971 through 1977 and before that for the years 1964 through 1966. Estimates for 1967–1970 were made by linear interpolation between 1966 and 1971. For the years 1961–1963 average monthly hours were reported but were presented only on an unweighted basis. Consequently I applied the ratio of weighted hours to unweighted hours for the years 1964–1966 to the unweighted hours from 1961 to 1963 to obtain figures comparable to the weighted average monthly hours. Finally, I assumed that scheduled average hours of operation from 1950 through 1963 would be a constant 342 hours per month, or

94

TABLE 46

UTILIZATION OF COMPUTERS IN THE FEDERAL GOVERNMENT, GENERAL MANAGEMENT CLASSIFICATION, FISCAL YEAR 1977

Computer Price Range ($)	Average Price of Computer ($)	Number of Systems	Aggregate Cost of Systems[a] ($ millions)	Monthly Scheduled Hours of Use
50,000 or less	30,000	638	19.14	253
50,001–200,000	125,000	828	103.50	326
200,001–500,000	350,000	678	237.30	420
500,001–1,500,000	1,000,000	591	591.00	499
More than 1,500,000	2,500,000	551	1,377.50	554
Total or average		3,286	2,328.44	(513.8)

a. Column 1 × column 2.

SOURCES: Columns 2 and 4 from General Services Administration. Column 1, author.

80 hours a week. Average monthly hours of computers from 1961 to 1977 are presented in column 1 of table 47.

Adjusting for Productivity Change. Column 1 of table 47 shows that hours worked by computers rose steadily from 1962 to 1974 and since then have declined irregularly. The moderate decline probably reflects the development of smaller, less costly computers, which are discussed elsewhere. I am concerned with the 52 percent increase in average monthly hours from 1961 to 1974, which is the equivalent of an annual rate of increase of 3.3 percent. This increase probably reflects not only the increased importance of large computers and their

TABLE 47

AVERAGE MONTHLY HOURS OF OPERATION OF COMPUTERS USED IN THE
FEDERAL GOVERNMENT, BEFORE AND AFTER ADJUSTMENT FOR
PRODUCTIVITY CHANGE, 1961–1977

Fiscal Year	Weighted Average Monthly Hours (1)	Hours Attributable to Productivity Increase (2)	Adjusted Monthly Hours (3)
1961	361	0.0	361
1962	327	3.6	323
1963	349	7.3	342
1964	372	10.9	361
1965	402	14.6	387
1966	422	18.4	404
1967	437	22.2	415
1968	453	26.0	427
1969	468	29.9	438
1970	484	33.8	450
1971	499	37.7	461
1972	516	41.7	474
1973	542	45.7	496
1974	549	49.8	499
1975	526	53.9	472
1976	540	58.1	482
1977	514	62.3	452

SOURCES: Column 1: see text. Column 2: starting with 1961 as a base, productivity growth was assumed to add 1 percent per year compounded to monthly hours. Column 3: column 1 minus column 2.

longer work schedules but also an increase in the productivity of management's use of their computers. One computer expert, Montgomery Phister, believes that for a computer of given cost there has been a rise in operating hours over the years.[1] He uses as an example a computer that worked 300 hours a month in 1960 and by 1978 worked 380 hours a month, which yields a compounded annual rate of growth of 1.32 percent. In my view this rise in hours would reflect two main factors: first, the familiarizing of personnel with the new equipment (a kind of learning by doing) and, second, the finding of new uses for the equipment.[2] Since this study is concerned with changes in weekly hours worked as a result of changing shifts and days worked per week, it seemed reasonable to make at least a rough adjustment for productivity growth that reflected greater familiarity with the equipment and new uses for the equipment. Therefore I subtracted 1 percent per annum growth in productivity from the figures in column 1 of table 47. The series after this adjustment (column 2) appears in the last column.

Estimating Average Hours Worked
by All Office Equipment, Including Computers

The large computers that operate multiple shifts are one part of the privately owned office equipment stock in which we are interested. The other part consists of all the more conventional types of office equipment that operate a single shift—typewriters, desk calculators, addressing machines, copying machines, and the like. Weighting the average hours of the two parts together should yield an estimate of average hours for all privately owned office and computing equipment. Our basic problem is to derive weights for these two parts.

Our first task is to estimate weights for the large computers whose hours are presented in table 47. This is accomplished in a series of steps described in tables 48, 49, and 50.

Table 48 shows the value of all computers in use in the United States, broken down into "general-purpose" and "other" computers. "General-purpose" refers to the larger machines used mostly for business data processing and scientific calculations. The "other" category is dominated by the smaller computers, referred to as minicomputers or minis. These estimates are from trade sources noted in the table because when this study was prepared the Bureau of Economic Analysis (BEA) did not have independent estimates of the gross stock of computers in the private sector; computers are subsumed under "office equipment." The figures from trade sources are extensively used, although Phister points out that they should be used with care.[3]

TABLE 48

ESTIMATED VALUE OF COMPUTERS IN USE IN THE UNITED STATES,
1950–1978
(billions of dollars)

	Total	General-Purpose	Other
1950	0.0	0.0	0.0
1951	0.0	0.0	0.0
1952	0.0	0.0	0.0
1953	0.1	0.1	0.0
1954	0.1	0.1	0.0
1955	0.2	0.2	0.0
1956	0.3	0.3	0.0
1957	0.5	0.5	0.0
1958	0.9	0.9	0.0
1959	1.3	1.3	0.0
1960	2.0	1.9	0.1
1961	2.7	2.6	0.1
1962	3.6	3.5	0.1
1963	4.8	4.6	0.2
1964	6.3	6.0	0.3
1965	8.1	7.8	0.3
1966	9.9	9.4	0.5
1967	13.1	12.4	0.7
1968	16.6	15.7	0.9
1969	20.3	19.1	1.2
1970	23.0	21.5	1.5
1971	25.1	23.3	1.8
1972	26.8	24.7	2.1
1973	29.9	27.3	2.6
1974	33.6	30.2	3.4
1975	37.9	33.8	4.1
1976	43.4	37.9	5.5
1977	50.4	42.9	7.5
1978	58.9	48.6	10.3

SOURCES: 1974–1978, EDP Industry Report, May 28, 1980, vol. 15, nos. 23, 24, International Data Corp.; 1966–1974, EDP Industry Report, April 19, 1974, vol. 9, no. 13; 1955–1966, EDP Industry Report, March 25, 1969, no. 14. Values of total and general-purpose computers appear with occasional minor variation in Montgomery Phister, Jr., *Data Processing Technology and Economics*, 2d ed. (Santa Monica, Calif: Santa Monica Publishing Co., 1979), 1955–1958, p. 251, lines 129, 109, and 1959–1978, pp. 600–601, lines 129, 109.

TABLE 49

Value of Computers in Use by Federal, State, and Local Governments, 1950–1978
(billions of dollars)

	Total Government			Federal Government			State and Local Government		
	Total	Owned	Leased	Total	Owned	Leased	Total	Owned	Leased
1950	0.00	0.00	0.00	0.00	0.00	0.00	0.00	0.00	0.00
1951	0.12	0.02	0.10	0.12	0.02	0.10	0.00	0.00	0.00
1952	0.24	0.04	0.20	0.24	0.04	0.20	0.00	0.00	0.00
1953	0.36	0.06	0.30	0.36	0.05	0.30	0.00	0.00	0.00
1954	0.47	0.07	0.40	0.47	0.07	0.40	0.00	0.00	0.00
1955	0.59	0.09	0.50	0.59	0.09	0.50	0.00	0.00	0.00
1956	0.71	0.11	0.60	0.71	0.11	0.60	0.00	0.00	0.00
1957	0.84	0.13	0.71	0.83	0.12	0.71	0.01	0.00	0.01
1958	0.97	0.14	0.83	0.95	0.14	0.81	0.02	0.00	0.02
1959	1.10	0.18	0.92	1.07	0.17	0.90	0.03	0.01	0.02
1960	1.24	0.19	1.05	1.19	0.18	1.10	0.05	0.01	0.04
1961	1.38	0.17	1.21	1.30	0.16	1.14	0.08	0.01	0.07
1962	1.53	0.21	1.32	1.42	0.20	1.23	0.11	0.01	0.10
1963	1.69	0.29	1.40	1.54	0.27	1.27	0.15	0.03	0.12
1964	1.87	0.61	1.26	1.66	0.54	1.12	0.21	0.07	0.14
1965	2.07	0.84	1.23	1.78	0.72	1.05	0.29	0.12	0.17
1966	2.28	0.99	1.29	1.90	0.82	1.07	0.38	0.16	0.22

(Table continues)

TABLE 49 (continued)

	Total Government			Federal Government			State and Local Government		
	Total	Owned	Leased	Total	Owned	Leased	Total	Owned	Leased
1967	2.54	1.19	1.35	2.02	0.95	1.07	0.52	0.24	0.28
1968	2.76	1.29	1.47	2.05	0.96	1.09	0.71	0.33	0.38
1969	3.29	1.60	1.69	2.36	1.15	1.21	0.93	0.45	0.48
1970	3.86	2.01	1.85	2.80	1.46	1.34	1.06	0.55	0.51
1971[a]	4.26	2.53	1.73	3.06	1.82	1.24	1.20	0.71	0.49
1972[a]	4.52	2.86	1.66	3.19	2.02	1.17	1.33	0.84	0.49
1973[a]	5.08	3.36	1.72	3.62	2.39	1.23	1.47	0.97	0.50
1974	5.79	3.98	1.80	4.04	2.78	1.26	1.75	1.20	0.55
1975	6.28	4.32	1.93	4.30	2.90	1.32	1.98	1.37	0.61
1976	6.80	4.80	2.00	4.41	3.11	1.30	2.39	1.69	0.70
1977	7.56	5.44	2.12	4.77	3.43	1.34	2.79	2.01	0.78
1978	7.91	5.71	2.20	4.89	3.53	1.36	3.02	2.18	0.84

a. Estimated for federal government in 1973 and for state and local governments in 1971 and 1972.

SOURCES: Federal: 1950–1967: 1950 assumed to be zero; subsequent years through 1966 obtained by linear interpolation. 1967–1972: Phister, *Data Processing Technology*, p. 451, line 30. 1973: interpolated. 1974–1978: General Services Administration. State and local: 1953–1972: Phister, p. 444, shows percentage of all general-purpose physical units that are in state and local governments for the years 1959, 1966, 1967, and 1969. Each year's percentage was multiplied ;by total dollar value of computers in place in the United States to obtain state adn local dollar value of computeres in place. Estimates for all other years, as well as for the years 1970–1972, were obtained by interpolation. Breakdown between owned and leased assumed same as federal. 1973–1978: based on Phister, *Data Processing Technology*, table II.3.11.1a, p. 652.

TABLE 50

ESTIMATED VALUE OF PRIVATELY OWNED COMPUTERS IN USE IN THE
UNITED STATES, 1953–1977
(billions of dollars)

	Total	General-Purpose	Other
1950	0		
1951	0		
1952	0		
1953	0	0.0	0.0
1954	0	0.0	0.0
1955	0.1	0.1	0.0
1956	0.2	0.2	0.0
1957	0.4	0.4	0.0
1958	0.8	0.8	0.0
1959	1.1	1.1	0.0
1960	1.8	1.7	0.1
1961	2.5	2.4	0.1
1962	3.4	3.3	0.1
1963	4.5	4.3	0.2
1964	5.7	5.4	0.3
1965	7.3	7.0	0.3
1966	8.9	8.5	0.4
1967	11.9	11.3	0.6
1968	15.3	14.5	0.8
1969	18.7	17.6	1.1
1970	21.0	19.6	1.4
1971	22.6	21.0	1.6
1972	23.9	22.0	1.9
1973	26.5	24.2	2.3
1974	29.6	26.6	3.0
1975	33.6	30.0	3.6
1976	38.6	33.7	4.9
1977	45.0	38.3	6.7

SOURCES: Column 1: U.S. total (column 1, table 48) minus government-owned (column 2, table 49). Columns 2 and 3: assumed same breakdown as in table 48.

TABLE 51

ESTIMATED VALUE OF STOCK OF PRIVATELY OWNED OFFICE EQUIPMENT, 1950–1976
(billions of 1972 dollars)

	Total Office Equipment (1)	Privately Owned Computers (2)	Equipment Excluding Computers (3)	Minicomputers (4)	Office Equipment Operating One Shift (5)
1950	4.5	a	4.5	a	4.5
1951	5.1	a	5.1	a	5.1
1952	5.6	a	5.6	a	5.6
1953	6.0	a	6.0	a	6.0
1954	6.4	a	6.4	a	6.4
1955	6.7	0.1	6.6	a	6.6
1956	7.1	0.2	6.9	a	6.9
1957	7.8	0.4	7.4	a	7.4
1958	8.4	0.8	7.6	a	7.6
1959	9.0	1.1	7.9	a	7.9
1960	9.7	1.8	7.9	0.1	8.0
1961			7.8	0.1	7.9

Year			
1962	7.7	0.1	7.8
1963	7.6	0.2	7.8
1964	7.5	0.3	7.8
1965	7.4	0.3	7.7
1966	7.3	0.4	7.7
1967	7.2	0.6	7.8
1968	7.1	0.8	7.9
1969	7.0	1.1	8.1
1970	6.9	1.4	8.3
1971	6.8	1.6	8.4
1972	6.7	1.9	8.6
1973	6.6	2.3	8.9
1974	6.5	3.0	9.5
1975	6.4	3.6	10.0
1976	6.3	4.9	11.2

a. Less than $50 million.

SOURCES: Column 1: Bureau of Economic Analysis, *Capital Stock Study*. Column 2: table 50, column (1). Column 3: column (1) − column (2) through 1960. Thereafter see text. Column 4: table 50, column (3). Column 5: column (3) + column (4).

TABLE 52

DERIVATION OF INDEX OF AVERAGE MONTHLY HOURS WORKED BY ONE-SHIFT OFFICE EQUIPMENT AND GENERAL-PURPOSE COMPUTERS, 1950–1976

	Conventional Equipment		Computers			Conventional Equipment plus Computers			
	Value (1972 $ billions) (1)	Aggregate hours (2)	Value (1972 $ billions) (3)	Average monthly hours (4)	Aggregate hours (5)	Value (1972 $ billions) (6)	Aggregate hours (7)	Average monthly hours (8)	Index of average monthly hours (9)
1950	4.5	778	0	342[a]	0	4.5	778	173	88.9
1951	5.1	882	0	342[a]	0	5.1	882	173	88.9
1952	5.6	969	0	342[a]	0	5.6	969	173	88.9
1953	6.0	1038	0	342[a]	0	6.0	1,038	173	88.9
1954	6.4	1107	0	342[a]	0	6.4	1,107	173	88.9
1955	6.6	1142	0.1	342[a]	0	6.7	1,142	170	87.4
1956	6.9	1194	0.2	342[a]	68	7.1	1,262	178	91.5
1957	7.4	1280	0.4	342[a]	137	7.8	1,417	182	93.5
1958	7.6	1315	0.8	342[a]	274	8.4	1,589	189	97.1

Year	(1)	(2)	(3)	(4)	(5)	(6)	(7)	(8)	(9)
1959	7.9	1367	1.1	342[a]	376	9.0	1,743	194	99.7
1960	8.0	1384	1.7	342[a]	581	9.7	1,965	203	104.3
1961	7.9	1367	2.4	361	866	10.3	2,233	217	111.5
1962	7.8	1349	3.3	323	1,066	11.1	2,415	218	112.0
1963	7.8	1349	4.3	342	1,471	12.1	2,820	233	119.7
1964	7.8	1349	5.4	361	1,949	13.2	3,298	250	128.5
1965	7.7	1332	7.0	387	2,709	14.7	4,041	275	141.3
1966	7.7	1332	8.5	404	3,434	16.2	4,766	294	151.1
1967	7.8	1349	11.3	415	4,690	19.1	6,039	316	162.4
1968	7.9	1367	14.5	427	6,192	22.4	7,559	337	173.2
1969	8.1	1401	17.6	438	7,709	25.7	9,110	354	181.9
1970	8.3	1436	19.6	450	8,820	27.9	10,256	368	189.1
1971	8.4	1453	21.0	461	9,681	29.4	11,134	379	194.8
1972	8.6	1488	22.0	474	10,428	30.6	11,916	389	199.9
1973	8.9	1540	24.2	496	12,003	33.1	13,543	409	210.2
1974	9.5	1644	26.6	499	13,273	36.1	14,917	413	212.2
1975	10.0	1730	30.0	472	14,160	40.0	15,890	397	204.0
1976	11.2	1938	33.7	482	16,243	44.9	18,181	405	208.1

a. Assumed the same throughout 1950–1960.

SOURCES: Column 1: table 51, column 5. Column 2: column 1 times 173 hours per month. Column 3: table 50, column 2. Column 4: table 47, last column. Column 5: column 3 times column 4. Column 6: column 1 plus column 3. Column 7: column 2 plus column 5. Column 8: column 7 divided by column 6. Column 9: index of column 8, 1929 = 100.

Table 48 refers to all computers, but our interest is in weights for the private sector. Table 49 shows the value of computers of federal, state, and local governments broken down into those computers owned and those leased. The notes attached to the tables show the sources for the various parts of the table.

Table 50 shows privately owned computers by type. Column 1 is obtained by subtracting all government-owned computers from the grand total in table 48. Computers owned by private firms but leased to the government are part of the privately owned stock. Table 50 also breaks down the private total into general-purpose and all-other computers. The proportions reflect those in table 48. The values of the stock of general-purpose computers constitute the weights for the time series on hours worked by the larger computers as shown in table 47. But this is only part of the story.

To estimate the rest of the stock, I started off with BEA estimates of the stock of all office equipment including computers.[4] I then subtracted the privately owned computers shown in table 50 to derive a noncomputer total, to which I added the minicomputers shown as "other" in table 50. The minicomputers are believed to operate a *single* shift since the need to economize on their use is greatly diminished by virtue of their relatively low capital cost. The sum of the conventional office equipment stock plus the stock of minicomputers should represent the total stock working a single shift.

In its capital stock series BEA assumes that prices of computers have remained unchanged since their introduction. Accepting this assumption means that current dollar estimates of computer stocks can be treated as constant dollar estimates as well. BEA estimates probably understate the value of the real computer stock and the stock of office equipment generally because prices are overstated. At first I accepted in part BEA's assumption of no price change for computers even though serious questions can be raised about its reasonableness.

Later I found it necessary to modify the previously explained procedure because it yielded an erratically behaving stock of conventional equipment. This is because my estimate of computers is free running, that is, it is not controlled by the BEA's estimates of office equipment and assumptions regarding computer prices. I believe that the stock of conventional office equipment is either stagnant or slowly declining because of the extremely rapid growth of computers in the office work field. Consequently, I decided arbitrarily to introduce a negative time trend into my conventional office equipment estimates starting after 1961 (− $100 million per year). I then added the minicomputers to this conventional series to derive the stock working a single shift. Estimates are shown in table 51. Estimates of the conventional equipment including the adjustment mentioned above are given in column 3.

Table 52 shows the derivation of average weekly hours for the office equipment total including computers. Starting in 1950 the conventional equipment is assumed to be subject to a work schedule of 173 hours per month (40 hours a week times 4.3 weeks) while the general-purpose computers are subject to a monthly hours schedule as shown in the last column of table 47.[5] Each is weighted by its annual stock to arrive at a time series of weighted average hours for all office equipment.

This particular series showed a strong rise to about 1973 and since then has essentially leveled off. This is because the working week or month of large general-purpose computers seems to have reached a peak and is no longer increasing. In addition, because of the rapid growth of minicomputers, the weight of the large computers in terms of value is not gaining at the expense of the stock that works a single shift.

For the years from 1929 to 1950 I decided to move the office equipment series by hours worked by the finance, insurance, and real estate industry, which is dominated by the experience of white-collar workers. This industry division series shows a decline of 6.6 percent from 1929 to 1940 and a further decline of 4.8 percent from 1940 to 1950.[6] The office equipment series as a whole shows a rise of 108 percent in average hours from 1929 to 1976 or an average compounded rise of 1.57 percent per year. From 1950 to 1976 the average annual rate of increase is 3.32 percent.

Notes

1. Montgomery Phister, Jr., *Data Processing Technology and Economics*, 2d ed. (Santa Monica, Calif.: Santa Monica Publishing Co., 1979) p. 510; p. 511, table 11.4.4.5; and p. 562, table 3.0.7a, line 13. Although the specific figures on monthly hours are assumptions, Phister's knowledge of computers is such that one can accept his assumptions as reasonable approximations of actual developments.

2. A British survey of business firms showed that five applications—financial accounting, invoicing and billing, management information services, payroll, and stock control—accounted for 89 percent of computer time in 1964 but only 76 percent five years later. Ibid., p. 437, table 11.3.12.2.

3. Ibid., p. 5.

4. Bureau of Economic Analysis, "Capital Stock Study," as updated February 1981, refers to "office, computing and accounting machinery." The stock estimates reflect useful lives equal to 85 percent of Internal Revenue Service, *Estimated Useful Lives and Depreciation Rates*, Bulletin F (January 1942).

5. The assumption that conventional office equipment was subject to an

unchanged 40-hour week from 1950 onward could possibly be a slight overstatement. On one hand, according to the BLS, average scheduled hours per week for office-clerical *workers* in all metropolitan areas were 39.0 hours in 1959–1960 and 38.7 hours in 1976, a total decrease of 0.8 percent over sixteen years. Moreover, average weekly hours in the finance, insurance, and real estate industry—a white-collar industry—fell by 1.3 percent from 1950 to 1960. It is thus conceivable that scheduled hours per week for equipment fell by 2 percent over this twenty-six-year period. On the other hand, there was undoubtedly a little shift work of perhaps eight hours per shift for some equipment like punchcard equipment and private switchboards. So the assumption of an unchanging 40-hour week is not unreasonable and in any case not likely to be very much off the mark.

6. This industry division series shows a further decline from 37.7 hours per week in 1950 to 36.4 hours in 1976. I ignored this change, however, because of my belief that the 40 hours per week is a reasonable figure for all office workers.

Appendix A

Final Estimates and Weights

Table 1 shows the indexes of average weekly capital hours for each industry division from 1929 to 1976 as well as for the total nonfarm business sector. The detailed estimating procedures used for industry divisions not discussed in the text are described in appendixes B, C, D, and E.

In putting together overall figures for the nonfarm economy, I used a set of fixed weights. The weights, the first row of figures in table 1, are BEA estimates of 1954 gross stocks of fixed nonresidential private business capital, excluding farm capital and that of nonprofit organizations, in 1972 prices and, within nonfarm nonmanufacturing, BLS estimates. Since the detailed industry estimates came from the BLS, however, it was necessary to make adjustments to BEA levels. This and other adjustments are described in this appendix. Appendix F shows the results of an alternative set of weights.

Continuous nonmanufacturing industries, where no change in weekly hours was assumed for the entire period, accounted for 48.5 percent of the weight in 1954. Manufacturing as a whole had a weight of 33.1 percent. Thus the industry divisions for which reasonably reliable estimates of capital hours were available were more than 80 percent of the 1954 weight.

Adjustments

1. Reallocation of Real Estate Industry. For purposes of constructing an index of the workweek of capital, it seems desirable to view capital on a user rather than on an owner basis. The BLS figures refer to assets owned by each industry rather than assets used. I reallocated the capital of the real estate industry excluding residential on the basis of estimated rentals paid; I made no attempt to reallocate rented equipment, a more difficult task.

From the BEA input-output table covering the year 1972 it was possible to obtain payments by each industry to the real estate and rental industry.[1] Adjustments were made where the payments seemed to be primarily for land. A percentage distribution of these adjusted payments was made and was multiplied by the capital (buildings and equipment) owned by the real estate and rental industry as estimated by the BLS. The results are an approximation of buildings rented and used by each industry. These results were added to the capital owned by each industry each year as estimated by the BLS.

2. Computer Adjustment. Since a separate synthetic industry was made for the activity of office equipment and computers, it was necessary to subtract such equipment from the stock of fixed capital in each industry. I assumed that stocks of all office equipment were proportional to the number of clerical and kindred workers as shown in the 1970 Census of Population for the experienced labor force. This procedure undoubtedly overweights industries using relatively few computers. The percentage distribution based on clerical and kindred workers was applied to $6.3 billion in office equipment stocks, which is the 1954 stock of such equipment in 1972 prices.

3. Difference between BEA and BLS Stocks. A final adjustment was necessary because BLS and BEA stocks differ. In 1954 BEA gross stocks showed the following relations to BLS gross stocks in 1972 prices.

	$BEA \div BLS$
Total nonfarm	1.094
Manufacturing	1.219
Other	1.048

BLS figures were adjusted upward by 21.9 percent for manufacturing and by 4.8 percent for all other industries.

Notes

1. See Philip M. Ritz, "The Input-Output Structure of the U.S. Economy, 1972," *Survey of Current Business*, vol. 59, no. 2 (February 1979), pp. 34–72. The real estate and rental industry is Industry 71 on this classification system.

Appendix B
Estimating Retail Store Hours

Following are the specific details regarding estimates of store hours in each kind of business.

1. General Merchandise, Apparel, and Furniture

Multi-unit. Sample of newspaper advertisements as described in text was used.

Single-unit. From 1929 to 1950—same movement was used as for multi-unit stores; thereafter, hours worked by self-employed.

2. Eating and Drinking Places. The Census Bureau published data in 1967 on hours open per day and days per week, but no comparable figures could be found for the other years.[1] For all outlets, hours per week were assumed to be unchanged over the entire period. This may not give proper recognition to fast-food places, many of which remain open all night.

3. Motor Vehicle Dealers. Hours of all outlets were assumed unchanged from 1929 to 1950; thereafter moved by hours worked by self-employed.

4. Lumber, Building Materials, and Hardware. Same general procedure was used as for motor vehicle dealers.

5. Gasoline Service Stations. A special survey conducted by National Analysts for E. I. duPont and Company Petroleum Chemical Division showed that weekly hours were ninety-nine in 1949. According to industry sources, small stations vary hours as a means of competing with company-owned stations. I assumed that hours rose from ninety in 1929 to ninety-five in 1940, then rose to ninety-nine in 1950, after which they are estimated to have remained flat. Since the oil crisis starting in late 1973 station hours have varied, becoming relatively short during the period of price controls and waiting lines, lengthening subsequently, shortening in 1979–1980 with the second round of major price increases, and then lengthening since that time.

6. All Other Retail except Food and Drug. Same general procedure was used as for motor vehicle dealers.

7. Food Stores

Multi-unit. It was possible to obtain store hours of supermarkets from *Progressive Grocer* (March or April issues) for the years 1954–1962, 1964, and 1971 forward. The 1954 figure was compared with a 1941 figure developed on the basis of data from *Chain Store Age*. Reflecting lengthening night hours and Sunday openings, this series shows a slow rise to the mid-1960s and an accelerated rise since then, with 1979 hours estimated at eighty-five per week. For the years 1929–1941 I assumed no change in hours; years not specified were obtained by interpolation.

Single-unit. For single-unit stores, weekly hours of the self-employed were used from 1950 to 1976. Hours from 1929 to 1951 were assumed to move with multi-unit hours, which meant no change from 1929 to 1941.

8. Drugstores. Eli Lilly and Company has provided annual estimates of weekly store hours maintained by independent drugstores from 1960 to 1967 and 1970 to 1976.[2] They show a rather steady decline from seventy-six to seventy-seven hours in 1960–1962 to sixty-five hours in 1976. I assumed that average hours were seventy-eight from 1929 through 1954. The same source (1968) showed that store hours per week varied by sales size, increasing from fifty-seven hours for stores with sales of $50,000 per year or less to eighty-five hours for stores with sales of $400,000 a year or more. I assumed that eighty-five was a reasonable approximation of average weekly store hours of multi-unit drugstores throughout the period.

Notes

1. For 1967 see U.S. Department of Commerce, Bureau of the Census, *1967 Census of Businesses, Retail Trade, Miscellaneous Subjects,* table 4, pp. 5–22.

2. 1970–1976: Letter from David J. Carter, ed., *Lilly Digest,* to author, July 28, 1978. Earlier years appear in various issues of *Lilly Digest,* published by Eli Lilly and Co., Indianapolis, Ind. Data are based on sample surveys.

Appendix C
Estimating Wholesale Trade Hours

Little information is available for wholesale trade, an industry division that in one sense can be thought of as falling between manufacturing, on the one hand, and retailing, on the other. Building design has been undergoing change toward economizing on floor space. Computers and forklift trucks have been used to an increasing extent.[1] Capital-output ratios have increased over the postwar period, and the proportion of single-unit firms has declined. For these reasons I felt that a small uptrend in average weekly hours would be warranted.

The BLS made a special tabulation of employment by shift of full-time wage and salary workers in May 1977 and May 1978 from the Current Population Survey. According to this tabulation, 9.1 percent of workers were employed on other than day shifts. Using the relation for manufacturing referred to in chapter 2 under "Translating Shift Proportions into Plant Hours" would yield an analogue to "plant hours" of sixty hours per week.

Using a totally different set of figures and approach, I came up with a similar figure. A recent study by the Department of Energy (DOE) shows hours of operation for different kinds and sizes of buildings.[2] According to this source, warehouse and storage buildings in the period October 1979–January 1980 operated 49.4 hours per week. In this particular calculation, however, each building is given equal weight. Buildings, of course, are not of equal size, and the same DOE study shows that hours of operation for buildings of all types vary directly with building size. These two pieces of information can be used to make better estimates of weekly hours for warehouses that would reflect size differences. The DOE study shows a frequency distribution of warehouse buildings by size. I assumed that what holds for buildings of all types holds also for warehouses, *so far as operating hours are concerned*. From this I derived a figure of 62.5 hours per week for warehouse and storage buildings, a figure that is close to the 60 hours per week indicated above.

113

Earlier data for comparison are virtually nonexistent. According to a BLS study of the storage and warehousing industry in July 1945, only 3 percent of the plant labor force was engaged in multiple-shift operations.[3] Although this survey is not strictly comparable with the 1977–1978 surveys showing 9 percent on late shifts, there is a strong suggestion of some upward trend. I arbitrarily decided to set the 1929 figure at fifty-six for multi-unit firms and to interpolate linearly between 1929 and 1976. For single-unit firms data on weekly hours of self-employed persons were available from 1950 forward. Average hours of single-unit firms before 1950 were assumed to be the same as in 1950.

Notes

1. Warren Blanding, "Storage and Warehousing," *Encyclopedia Britannica*, 15th ed. (Chicago: Helen Hemingway Benton, 1977), vol. 17, pp. 708–13.

2. U.S. Department of Energy, *Nonresidential Buildings Energy Consumption Survey: Building Characteristics*, DOE/EIA–0246 (March 1981).

3. U.S. Department of Labor, Bureau of Labor Statistics, *Wage Structure*, series 2, no. 24, 1945.

Appendix D

Estimating Services Industry Hours

Auto and Nonauto Repair Services

1950–1976. Hours worked by self-employed persons (as shown in special tabulations) were used in much the same way as described in retail trade.

1929–1950. Hours were assumed unchanged. To some extent they would be related to retail store hours, which were estimated to be unchanged over this period.

Business Services. If the average workweek of *labor* has declined over the long run in the average business, which is small, then the length of the workweek of the typical business has also declined. Firms providing services to business probably work a shorter week for the same reason; computer services are an important exception, but these are handled differently. Much of the activity here would be white-collar work. For this I used a Denison series on actual average weekly hours of full-time male wage and salary workers.[1]

Personal Services

1950–1976. Hours worked by self-employed persons were used as described in retail trade.

1929–1950. Hours were assumed to be unchanged. Many of these businesses, like barber shops, beauty parlors, and so forth, would tend to follow retail store hours, which are essentially unchanged over this period.

Amusements and Recreation. Average weekly hours were assumed to be unchanged throughout the period. Although this assumption may fail to allow for some rise in hours, there is little basis for making an adjustment. On one hand, increased leisure due to a shorter workday and workweek for labor ought to mean a longer workweek for amusement and recreation places generally. Working in the same direction would be the repeal of blue laws prohibiting or limiting sports on Sunday and the changed attitude of the public toward Sunday activity. On the other hand, some activities, like bowling alleys, amusement parks, golf courses, and so forth, have not changed much over the years.

All Other Services except Hospitals and Hotels. This group consists of industries like professional services (for example, doctors, dentists, lawyers), private for-profit schools and colleges, medical laboratories, and so forth. I decided to move this series by estimated hours worked by self-employed doctors, for which I had some census estimates (1950, 1960, and 1970) and Current Population Survey estimates for 1977. Weekly hours were assumed to be unchanged from 1929 to 1950.

Notes

1. Edward F. Denison, *Accounting for Slower Economic Growth: The United States in the 1970s* (Washington, D.C.: Brookings Institution, 1979), p. 196, table L–2.

Appendix E

Estimating Construction, Finance, and Communications Other Than Telephone Industry Hours

Shift work is uncommon in construction although it has always been used in heavy engineering projects. Average weekly equipment hours were assumed to move in the same fashion as average weekly labor hours. For the latter I used the BLS data on weekly hours for all trades from *Union Wages and Hours: Building Trades*.[1] Average weekly hours show a decline of 11.5 percent from 1929 to 1939 and essentially a flat trend thereafter.

Finance, real estate, and insurance are largely a reflection of the use of buildings and of office equipment other than computers since computers are given special treatment in this study. Consequently, a series showing hours worked by office employees should adequately reflect capital utilization by this group. A recent innovation is the increased use by banks of automated teller machines, which are available on a twenty-four-hour basis. According to an industry expert, there might have been some 14,000 installations of this kind in the fourth quarter of 1980, and at a cost of $40,000 per unit in current prices the value of such installations might exceed $0.5 billion.[2] This amount, however, is extremely small in relation to total fixed capital, and I decided not to make an adjustment on this account.

For the period 1947–1976 I used average weekly labor hours in finance, insurance, and real estate as shown by the BLS.[3] For years before 1947 I used Kendrick's estimates of weekly labor hours, except that I omitted his 1937 figure.[4] These data show a decline of 10.5 percent from 1929 to 1948 and then a downward drift of 4 percent from 1948 to 1978.

Television and Radio. Television stations operate longer hours now than they did thirty years ago, and radio stations broadcast more hours than they did fifty years ago. These longer operating hours are in part a reflection of listeners' habits, but they also may reflect a

117

desire on the part of station owners to use their capital more intensively.

Since 1970 the Federal Communications Commission has published tabulations of the number of minutes per week for all stations licensed in the United States. The unweighted average for 702 stations in 1976 was 7,720 minutes, or 128.7 hours, per week.[5] This average was extrapolated back to 1953 using sample data from a small number of large cities as shown below:

	Period	Change in Hours (%)
5 cities, 17 stations	1953–1960	14.4
7 cities, 22 stations	1960–1970	5.6
6 cities, 19 stations	1970–1976	3.4
	1953–1976	24.9

The sample data shown above were collated from issues of *TV Guide* available in the Library of Congress. Originally eight cities—Chicago, Cleveland, Detroit, Los Angeles, Miami, New York, Philadelphia, and St. Louis—were chosen, but the files were not available on a consistent basis. The data reflect changes for identical stations in the periods specified. An attempt was made to sample the three main stations in each city, except for Chicago, where four stations were used. In all cases the figures refer to hours of operation in the last week in June of each year.

For radio I used changes in the broadcasting day for New York City stations. For 1929–1940 the change was 13.0 percent, and for 1940–1953 I estimated the change thus obtained to be 5 percent. The changes from 1929 to 1953 for radio obtained in this fashion were linked to the changes from 1953 to 1976 for television, to yield an overall change of 48 percent.

Notes

1. U.S. Department of Labor, Bureau of Labor Statistics, *Union Wages and Hours: Building Trades*, Bulletin 1709 (July 1, 1970), and subsequent issues of this annual survey.

2. Telephone conversation with Linda Fenner Zimmer. See also her article "ATM Installations Surge," in *Magazine of Bank Administration* (May 1980), pp. 29–42.

3. BLS, *Employment and Earnings, United States, 1909–78*, Bulletin 1312–11.

4. John W. Kendrick, *Productivity Trends in the United States* (Princeton, N.J.: Princeton University Press for National Bureau of Economic Research, 1961), p. 310, table A-IX.

5. Federal Communications Commission, "Annual Programming Report for Commercial Television Stations," mimeographed (Washington, D.C., 1976).

Appendix F
Variable Weights and Their Effect on the All-Industry Results

The estimates in table 1 reflect the use of fixed 1954 weights, but I also made a set of estimates for the total nonfarm sector in which weights were permitted to vary. In the variable system four different periods are recognized, with weighting years as follows:

Period	Weight Year
1929–1948	average of 1929 and 1948
1948–1959	1954
1959–1969	1964
1969–1976	1972

Percentage distributions of the weights are given in table 53. Using more current weights starting in 1969—using 1972 rather than 1954 as the weight year—reduces the weight for manufacturing and increases it for services and finance. The continuous nonmanufacturing sector is also decreased. Office equipment more than doubles in relative importance but is still quite small on the basis of the BEA's figures.

With variable weights the all-industry results—average annual percentage changes in average weekly hours of fixed capital—show slightly faster growth in the postwar period, as the data below indicate:

	1929–1976	1929–1948	1948–1976
Fixed weights	0.18	0.18	0.19
Shifting weights	0.19	0.16	0.21

In manufacturing growth rates of weekly hours were a bit faster from 1948 to 1976 with shifting weights (0.41 percent per year versus 0.38 percent) because the weight of noncontinuous manufacturing industries employing shifts increases over this period. For all nonfarm business the rise in the weight of computers and office equipment also

TABLE 53

DISTRIBUTION OF FIXED CAPITAL WEIGHTS FOR NONFARM BUSINESS,
1929–1948, 1954, 1964, AND 1972

(percent)

	1929–1948 (average)	1954	1964	1972
Manufacturing	30.7	33.1	30.9	29.1
Mining[a]	1.5	1.0	1.4	1.7
Construction	1.0	1.3	2.0	1.9
Wholesale	1.5	1.8	2.0	2.7
Retail	4.7	6.0	7.3	7.8
Services	5.4	5.5	7.0	8.2
Finance and insurance	2.0	1.9	2.6	3.6
Television and radio	0.1	0.1	0.2	0.3
Continuous nonmanufacturing	52.3	48.5	45.2	42.6
Office equipment	0.8	0.8	1.4	2.1
Total nonfarm business	100.0	100.0	100.0	100.0

a. Excludes crude petroleum.

SOURCES: The calculation for 1954 is described in appendix A; 1964 and 1972 were calculated in similar fashion. The 1929–1948 average is based on percentage distributions of net stocks rather than of gross stocks, chiefly from Kendrick, *Productivity Trends in the United States*. In all cases stock estimates were adjusted to BEA levels for manufacturing and nonfarm nonmanufacturing.

contributed to the overall acceleration, as did the decline in the weight of the continuous nonmanufacturing group. The rapid growth of capital in services and finance, where weekly capital hours have decreased, partly offset these increases.

Appendix G
Capital-Labor Ratios

Capital-labor ratios[1] are measured much better when shift work can be taken into account.[2] Suppose Industry A employed 100 units of capital and 50 units of labor on a single shift, while Industry B employed the same aggregate quantities of capital and labor but on two shifts. Each worker in Industry A has two units of capital, but each worker in Industry B has four units. In the absence of shift information there is no way of distinguishing these two cases, with respect either to level or to change.

Figure 3 illustrates two measures of the ratio of capital to labor in manufacturing for the period 1948–1976. The lower line refers to all manufacturing industries and all production worker employment. It is a conventional measure. An alternative has a distinctly steeper trend.

For labor we started off with total production worker employment in manufacturing as published by the BLS and subtracted employment in one-shift industries and continuous industries.[3] The residual is the same as all-other manufacturing shown in table 13. Table 13 also gives figures on the proportion of workers in all-other manufacturing who work on late shifts and, by definition, on the first shift. Intervening years not shown in table 13 were obtained by interpolation. These ratios were applied to the all-other manufacturing employment totals to yield the number of production workers on the first shift.

For capital we started with estimated gross capital stocks in 1972 prices as estimated by the BLS[4] and made subtractions like those described for employment to obtain all-other manufacturing capital. The ratio of all-other manufacturing capital to total manufacturing capital as estimated by the BLS was then applied to BEA estimates of gross capital stocks, the assumption being that differences between the BLS and the BEA series of gross capital stocks affect all industries equally.[5] The capital figures obtained were divided by the first-shift employment figures to yield the data plotted with the solid line.

Table 54 compares growth rates in capital-labor ratios from 1948 to

TABLE 54

Capital-Labor Ratios and Their Growth, by Shift Characteristics of Industry, 1948 and 1976

	All Manufacturing	Continuous	One-Shift	All-Other
1948				
(1) Employment[a]	12,910	1,260	1,732	9,918
(2) Percentage on first shift	78.4	57.4	100.0	77.3
(3) Employment first shift[a]	10,122	723	1,732	7,667
(4) Capital stock[b]	179.9	64.2	4.4	111.2
Capital-labor ratios:				
(5) Line 4 ÷ line 3	17.77	88.8	2.5	14.5
(6) Line 4 ÷ line 1	13.93	51.0	2.5	11.2
1976				
(7) Employment[a]	13,638	1,121	1,725	10,792
(8) Percentage on first shift	72.0	57.4	100.0	69.0
(9) Employment first shift[a]	9,814	643	1,725	7,446
(10) Capital stock[b]	433.6	131.3	10.0	292.4

Capital-labor ratios:				
(11) Line 10 ÷ line 9	44.18	204.2	5.8	39.3
(12) Line 10 ÷ line 7	31.79	117.1	5.8	27.1
Annual growth rates in capital-labor ratios				
(13) Capital-first shift employment (line 11 versus line 5)	3.31	3.02	3.05	3.62
(14) Capital-total employment (line 12 versus line 6)	2.99	3.01	3.05	3.21

NOTE: Labor reflects employment of production workers only.

a. Production workers, in thousands.

b. Gross stocks in billions of 1972 dollars. BLS levels adjusted to BEA manufacturing totals.

SOURCE: See text of this appendix, including notes.

FIGURE 3

Two Measures of the Ratio of Fixed Capital to Production Worker Employment in Manufacturing, 1948–1976

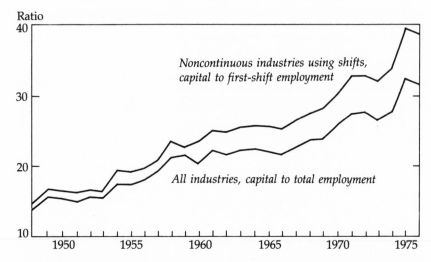

Ratio

Noncontinuous industries using shifts, capital to first-shift employment

All industries, capital to total employment

SOURCES: Ratios based on data from Bureau of Economic Analysis (capital) and Bureau of Labor Statistics (employment).

1976 when shifts are taken into account with rates computed when they are not. For all manufacturing the growth rate in the capital-labor ratio taking account of shifts is 3.31 percent per year as against 2.99 percent when shifts are ignored. A breakdown into the three groups—continuous, one-shift, and all-other manufacturing—shows that the growth rates for the continuous and one-shift groups were about equal over the twenty-eight years but that both were well below the 3.62 percent rate for all-other manufacturing.

Notes

1. This approach is a variant of the subject discussed in chapter 1. In this appendix, however, employment is confined to production workers, whose numbers have risen relatively less than those of all employees.

2. See Roger R. Betancourt and Christopher K. Clague, *Capital Utilization: A Theoretical and Empirical Analysis* (New York: Cambridge University Press, 1981), p. 3.

3. Bureau of Labor Statistics, *Employment and Earnings, United States, 1909–78*, Bulletin 1312–11 (1979), and *Supplement to Employment and Earnings, Revised Establishment Data* (August 1981).

4. BLS, *Capital Stock Estimates for Input-Output Industries: Methods and Data,* Bulletin 2034 (1979), p. 27.

5. John Musgrave, "Fixed Capital Stocks in the United States: Revised Estimates," *Survey of Current Business,* vol. 61 (February 1981), p. 59.

Appendix H

TABLE 55

Percentage of Production Workers on Late Shifts Compared with Average Weekly Plant Hours, Selected Industries, 1969–1980

Standard Industrial Classification Code	Industry	Date	% of Production Workers			Average Weekly Plant Hours (4th quarter 1976)
			2d shift	3d shift	Total	
2011	Meat packing	3/74 & 5/79	13.9	2.1	16.0	56.2
2013	Meat products	3/74 & 5/79	13.7	2.5	16.2	64.5
2065	Candy	8/75	20.0	4.0	24.0	68.8
2111	Cigarettes	5/76	32.9	16.5	49.4	106.5
221–2	Cotton & synthetic fabrics	5/75	29.4	23.6	53.0	127.0
223, 2283	Wool yarns & fabrics	5/75	24.8	14.9	39.7	87.0[a]
2251	Women's hosiery	7/76	13.6	5.1	18.7	96.9
2252	Other hosiery	7/76	14.8	5.0	19.8	88.2
226	Textile dyeing	6/76	26.7	14.8	41.5	109.0
2321	Men's shirts, etc.	6/74	n.a.	n.a.	4.0[b]	40.2
2327	Men's trousers	6/74	n.a.	n.a.	1.5	40.0
242	Southern sawmills[c]	10/69	n.a.	n.a.	6.0	57.0
2511	Wood household furniture	11/74	n.a.	n.a.	4.0[b]	45.1

SIC	Industry	Date			
2853	Corrugated bags	3/76	29.7	5.2	34.9	91.8
283	Drugs	10/80	19.8	5.9	25.7	85.2
2851	Paints & varnishes	11/76	11.2	2.9	14.1	69.1
3079	Misc. plastics	9/74	23.6	17.4	41.0	105.0
3111	Leather tanning	3/73	12.5	3.9	16.4	48.5
3141	Footwear	4/75	n.a.	n.a.	0	41.2
3251	Brick & clay tile	9/75	7.6	3.2	10.8	71.0
3253	Ceramic tile	9/75	14.0	2.5	16.5	91.2
3255	Clay refractories	9/75	18.0	7.7	25.7	66.7
3320	Iron & steel foundries	11/73 & 9/79	26.0	11.0	37.0	70.5
336	Nonferrous foundries	5/75	18.2	4.4	22.6	82.0
3441	Fabricated structural steel	11/74	15.3	1.4	16.7	62.5
3465	Auto stampings	4/74	28.2	3.8	32.0	101.2
35	Machinery[d]	1/78	19.4	4.6	24.0	80.0
3592	Auto pistons, etc.	4/74	30.5	8.6	39.1	97.7
3674	Semiconductors	9/77	27.0	14.2	41.2	86.2
3694	Engine electrical equipment	4/74	18.1	3.6	21.7	101.4
3731	Shipbuilding	9/76	21.7	8.4	30.1	97.0

n.a. = not available.

a. Combination of wool yarns (weighted 1) and wool fabric (weighted 3).

b. "Less than 5 percent"—the reference in the BLS text—was assumed to be 4 percent.

c. West Coast late-shift proportion also 6.0 percent.

d. Derived from individual SMSA data weighted together by employment. Calculations by author.

SOURCES: Bureau of Labor Statistics, "Industry Wage Surveys"; and Bureau of the Census, "Survey of Plant Capacity" (special tabulations).

Appendix I

TABLE 56

VARIABLES USED IN REGRESSION ON AVERAGE WEEKLY PLANT HOURS IN
ALL-OTHER MANUFACTURING, 1948–1976

	Capital-Labor Ratio	Wage Differential	Percentage of Manufacturing Capital in South	Percentage of Manufacturing Output in Single Units	Index of Average Weekly Plant Hours
1948	14.52	3.8	23.6	39.5	116.7
1949	16.48	3.9	23.6	38.3	116.8
1950	16.27	3.9	23.6	37.0	117.0
1951	16.22	4.0	23.6	35.8	117.1
1952	16.78	4.1	23.6	34.5	117.3
1953	16.61	4.2	23.6	33.3	117.6
1954	18.93	4.3	23.6	32.0	117.8
1955	19.07	4.4	23.9	30.6	118.1
1956	19.75	4.5	24.1	29.2	118.4
1957	20.80	4.5	24.4	27.8	118.7
1958	22.87	4.6	25.0	26.4	118.8
1959	22.37	4.7	25.6	25.9	119.1
1960	22.91	4.8	26.1	25.3	119.1
1961	24.20	4.7	26.7	24.8	120.2
1962	24.31	4.6	27.2	24.2	121.2
1963	24.83	4.6	27.3	23.7	122.2
1964	25.39	4.5	27.2	22.8	123.2
1965	25.38	4.5	27.8	21.8	124.3
1966	25.24	4.5	28.3	20.9	125.3
1967	26.59	4.4	28.9	20.0	126.4
1968	27.53	4.4	29.1	19.8	127.3
1969	28.23	4.5	29.4	19.7	128.4
1970	30.57	4.5	29.8	19.5	129.0
1971	32.20	4.4	30.3	19.4	129.4
1972	32.16	4.4	31.0	19.2	130.0
1973	31.78	4.2	31.7	18.8	130.7
1974	33.34	4.1	32.4	18.4	131.1
1975	37.62	3.9	33.1	17.9	131.7
1976	37.38	4.1	34.1	17.5	132.4

SOURCE: See chap. 3 of text, "Regressions."